THE LANGUAGE
OF
THE CROSS

THE LANGUAGE
OF
THE CROSS

edited by
Aelred Lacomara C.P.

FRANCISCAN HERALD PRESS
1434 WEST 51st STREET ● CHICAGO, 60609

The Language of the Cross edited by Aelred Lacomara C.P., copyright©1977, Franciscan Hearld Press, 1434 West 51st Street, Chicago, Illinois 60609. Made in the United States of America. All rights reserved.

Library of Congress Cataloging in Publication Data:

Main entry under title:

The Language of the cross.
    1. Jesus Christ—Passion—Addresses, essays, lectures. 2. Suffering—Addresses, essays, lectures.   I. Lacomara, Aelred.
BT431.L37   232.9'63   76-43287
ISBN 0-8199-0617-4

IMPRIMI POTEST:
  Very Rev. Flavian Dougherty, C.P.
  Provincial Superior
  Province of St. Paul of the Cross

NIHIL OBSTAT:
  Rev. William F. Hogan
  Censor Librorum

IMPRIMATUR:
  +Most Rev. Thomas A. Boland, S.T.D.
  Archbishop of Newark

January 5, 1977

INTRODUCTION

On October 19th, 1975, the Passionist Congregation began a special year of grace and reflection to commemorate the two-hundredth anniversary of the death of its Founder, St. Paul of the Cross.

Paul of the Cross, as his name indicates, was gifted with an extraordinary mystical knowledge and love for Jesus Crucified. That love led him particularly to found a Community whose members would attempt to share his special gift in living in deep prayer on the Passion and communicating the message of the Cross to others.

The following studies are a special gift from some of the Scripture scholars in the Passionist family to honor our father in Christ.

These articles study the message of the Cross as foreshadowed in the Old Testament, as presented from the viewpoint of each of the Gospel writers, and as applied to the Christian life in the Epistles of St. Paul. They can nourish our understanding and re-enkindle the flame of faith.

Sincere thanks are due to the Passionist scholars who prepared these studies as a tribute to their father and founder, St. Paul of the Cross. They surely have thus continued his urgent work of promoting devotion to the Passion of the Son of God.

May the Passion of Jesus Christ be always in our hearts, so that the life also of Jesus may be in us!

Flavian Dougherty C.P.
Provincial

CONTENTS

Faith and Abandonment
in the
Psalms of Supplication

Carroll Stuhlmueller C.P.
Catholic Theological Union
Chicago, Illinois

MYSTICS, like the Saints of the Cross, John and Paul, confess to have been exquisitely at peace in God when they were plunged into the agony of divine abandonment. John of the Cross wrote:

> Job, with his wounds, clearly beheld this marvel when he said to God: *Returning to me, You torment me wondrously.* Job 10:16. This is an unspeakable marvel and worthy of the abundance and sweetness God has hidden for them that fear him. Ps. 30:20: to cause a person to enjoy so much the more savor and sweetness, the more pain and torment he experiences. [*The Living Flame of Love,* stanza 2, n. 13, trans. K. Kavanaugh and O. Rodriguez (Washington, D.C., 1973), p. 600]

This statement of John of the Cross illumines for us the long period of abandonment suffered by Paul of the Cross.

In this essay, however, we turn to the Holy Scriptures, the common source of spirituality for both these saints. In particular, we seek enlightenment from the "psalms of supplication" to guide us into the painful yet peaceful way of faith and atonement.

The path of the cross, trod by Jesus and his follower, Paul of the Cross, seemed to be a road plummeting into dark depths away from God. Yet with Jesus, as with his saints, and hopefully with ourselves, never is God *the Redeemer* so manifest as along that sacred way. Each step is possible only through the strength and direction provided by the divine Redeemer.

3

The most abandoned moment of life turns into the most radiant act of deliverance. Each new death turns into a new resurrection. The cry of desperation is over-taken almost immediately by the shout of Hallelujah, which in turn is drowned out by new moments of loss.

In fact, to appreciate the prayers of supplication in the Psalter, we best begin by comparing them with the hymns of praise to God, gloriously and joyfully present as Redeemer. Despite serious and inherent differences, both types of psalms share a *similar literary structure* and are unified, basically, in the *one faith* of Israel in God as Redeemer. The literary forms of both types can be compared thus:

	Hymns of Praise	*Prayers of Supplication*
Introduction	(Pss. 8, 19, 29, 104) Call to praise and worship God	(Pss. 12, 22, 69) Call to God for help
Central part	Motivation for praise by recalling and reliving God's great redemptive acts *now*. Not the reason *why*, but the wondrous acclamation "Indeed!"	Expression of pain, abandonment by God, and hatred of enemy; petitions for help; but *not* the reason why God allows suffering
Conclusion	Repetition of the call to praise	Repetition of the call for help or anticipated thanksgiving

In this schematic presentation, which points out a similarity in literary form between the hymn and the prayer, one will also notice *a common, basic attitude of faith* in the central section of each. Neither type pro-gresses logically with human reasons; instead, each re-mains for the most part in the faith that God is pres-ent. This conviction, called faith, cannot be proved or even adequately explained; it must be experienced. Because the encounter with God happens at a profound depth within the human psyche and with such intensity, it bursts the confines of grammatical sentences and rational words. In view of this innate force, which seizes the soul, a person remains in wonder or in agony, or both. Solace or relief comes much more in the sheer ability to sustain this experience than in the intellectual satisfaction of explaining it.

To appreciate the faith of the psalmist when he is confronted with suffering, we must do what he (or she) never did: seek some reasons and attempt some explanation. As background to the prayers of supplication in the Psalter, our first major section will discuss (1) various aspects of Israel's faith in God during suffering, (2) the absence of any sacred liturgy for sickness and death, and (3) the difficult question of associating suffering with sin. All three topics are raised by a statement or attitude, continuing from the Old Testament into the New, that Yahweh is the God of the living, not of the dead (cf. Gen 2:7; Ex 3:6; Ez 37:1-14; Matt 22:32). Then, in the second major section, we will join Israel at prayer and study several individual psalms of supplication.

Part 1. The Theological Context for Suffering and Death

A God of Life

In the Psalter, suffering is never identified with God. In fact, pain remains a mystery, irreconcilable with God. The suffering prisoner, composing Psalm 22, asks with poignant amazement, even in broken grammar: "My God! My God! Why have you abandoned me? Far from my salvation (be) the roar of my words!"

Divine goodness remains the basic ingredient in the

mysticism of the psalms; only it is present differently. In the hymns of praise, the psalmist is swept *beyond* words in the wonder of God's goodness, while in the prayers of supplication, pain has left the worshiper so far *behind* this goodness as again to be speechless!

Israel staunchly confessed that Yahweh not only lives, but can be acclaimed as "a compassionate and gracious God, slow to anger and rich in kindness and fidelity" (Ex 34:6-7). Moreover, if the word *Yahweh* is to be explained as "he who is always there" (following such European scholars as W. Eichrodt and G. von Rad), then he must be present as he really is, a Redeemer who is kind, gracious, and forgiving, driving away pain and threats to life.

Israel, consequently, could not countenance a god of suffering or a god of death. Canaanites even named one of their gods Muth or Moth, which is the normal Hebrew-Canaanite word for "death." The mythologies of the ancient Near East possessed stories about the gods' dying and rising again. These myths were actually a rationalistic explanation, personalistic and pre-scientific, but all the while highly intellectual, for answering the problem of how suffering and joy, death and life can co-exist. There were separate gods for each experience, or at least separate moments in the career of a single god.

Israel never resorted to such rationalistic subterfuges. She confessed that Yahweh was *always there,* present with the full force of his life and goodness, even when she could not say how, even when she felt obliged to cry out to an absent God and yet believe that her cry was heard!

A final comment, better described as a digression, is that Israel could *implicitly accept* what she *explicitly denied.*

In Psalm 22, a distant God, who is said. to have abandoned his people, is still considered near enough to hear and be concerned about the cry of his people. Again, in many passages, such as Psalms 6:6, 30:10, 88:11-12, 113:17, and Is 38:18, we read the lament that the dead cannot praise God or even contact him. Yet all the while, Isreal confessed that Yahweh's gracious fidelity was stronger than even the blood bond within a family. Isaiah wrote in this context: "Fathers declare to their sons, O God, your faithfulness" (38:19). Again, this same faith, looking into the mysterious face of death, was left without an answer: "For among the dead no one remembers you nor . . . gives you thanks" (Ps 6:6)

When these tests are put together, it seems that what the Bible denies explicitly it also maintains at least implicitly.

No Sacred Liturgy for Death

Israel possessed a very elaborate ritual of mourning for the dead (too extensive to describe here). As a result, professional mourners, sometimes very jealous of their position (cf. Matt 9:24), could be hired so as to conduct the service properly. Yet the ritual remained entirely profane, outside the realm of sacred liturgical ceremonies.

The classic and moving elegies of Israel's literature, like David's lament over Saul and Jonathan, do not mention the name of God! (2 Sam 1:19-27). Moreover, the high priest, as the one closest to Yahweh and most representative of God's presence, was not permitted to mourn the death of even his father and mother (Lev 21:1). All other priests, moreover, though granted some exceptions, must obey the prescript: "None of you shall render himself unclean for any dead person among his people" (Lev 21:1). Contact with a corpse—even to be present in the same house with it—rendered a person unclean for sanctuary worship. These laws, found in the Priestly Tradition of the Pentateuch, reflect a postexilic spirituality and not just an early "superstitious" stage. Even today, on the Mount of Olives in Israel, an elaborate system of Hebrew signs directs the path of the *Kohanim* or priests so that they will not inadvertently defile themselves by any of the cemeteries on the mountain.

Death remained outside the sanctuary of the living God. Very consistently, then, slaughtering an animal for sacrifice was by no means a sacred act. The ritual in the early chapters of Leviticus relegates the killing of the animal to the lay person who brings this offering. Slaughtering was necessary, but the act was not sacred—no more than it is an accepted topic of conversation at the family dinner table. The lay person, having killed the victim and carefully drained the blood from the corpse, presented them to the priest, who then initiated the sanctuary ritual. Blood, we note, was never offered to God. As symbolic of *life* and the unity of life among the many members of the one body, blood was sprinkled on the altar, and at times on the people, to announce and thereby intensify the oneness of life and holiness in the community with God, or to manifest that sin was forgiven and reunion with God achieved (cf. Lev 17:11; Ex 24:5-8; Lev 16).

This discussion of life and death in relation to the Israelite liturgy brings our discussion to the delicate and important topic of atonement. Leviticus 17:11 summarizes it thus:

> Since the life of the living body is in its blood, I have made you put it on the altar, so that atonement may thereby be made for your own lives, because it is the blood, *as the seat of life,* that makes atonement.

"Blood . . . makes atonement" in that it instills, maintains, and strengthens life where life has become weak or is threatened with death. Atonement is achieved when those with "good" blood, most of all God, unite with others in need of purer blood to expel disease. One person's health cannot substitute for another's bad health. Only in the closest bond of life—through a blood transfusion—can one healthy member of the body come to the aid of another sick member.

At-one-ment is achieved by union, not by substitution. Strictly speaking, therefore, Jesus did not suffer or die for us—that is, in place of us—because we still suffer and must die. By suffering and dying, Jesus united himself with *our* suffering and *our* dying, and in that most initimate bond, his obedience to the Father's will and oneness of glorious life with the Father surge through us, and we rise to a newness of life in his resurrection (cf. Rom 6:1–14).

In the psalms of supplication, we find a union of the saint and the sinner, of the living and the dead, of the suffering and the joyful, of faith and desperation. Because the psalmist believed, he had problems with his faith; and because he believed firmly, he absolutely would not accept evil. Because he believed with love, he was compelled to cry out to God, who had seemingly abandoned him. Let us listen to the words in Psalm 22, revealing the inexplicable, mystic nearness of a distant God.

My God! My God! Why have you abandoned me?
Far from my salvation be the roar of my words!
O my God, I cry out day by day, and you answer not;
night by night, and there is no relief for me.
Yet you are the one enthroned in the holy place,
O glory of Israel!
In you our fathers trusted;
they trusted, and you delivered them.
To you they cried, and they escaped;
in you they trusted, and they were not put to shame.
But I am a worm, not a man . . .
Be not far from me, for distress is near;
I have no one to help me.

Converging in this psalm are all the real components, good and bad, of the Israelite community. Because the psalmist was plunged so totally into the lives of sinful people, he suffered, and he suffered more fiercely because of his greater goodness. Yet this goodness produced a psalm which would sustain the discouraged and purify the sinful down through the ages, until Jesus himself took refuge within its words. Once again we find the example of atonement by union, whereby goodness, submerged within evil, provides the strength of new blood to purify the evil, revivify the person, and achieve the new resurrection.

Sin in Relation to Suffering

Biblically, sin is removed not by the good person's substituting his or her suffering for the wickedness of the evil person but by uniting himself or herself so closely with the sinner that goodness drives out wickedness and all are purified. This process of purification does not preclude suffering. Forgiveness, suffusing an ever greater goodness within the soul of the sinner, causes *more* suffering.

An example may help us understand this last statement. An otherwise healthy person, with strong vital
organs, suffers far more from poison in the system than
someone with a bad heart, poor circulation, weal lungs,
and failing kidneys and spleen. The latter can quickly
lapse into a comatose situation and suffer very little.
Applying this example to theology, we find that goodness causes ever more suffering within a person or a
community, for it strengthens the body to eject evil
ever more vigorously. A loving and faithful spouse suffers more from an unfriendly word than a playboy feels
from adultery.

Suffering, then, is not so much punishment as purification. The silence of God's leaving the sinner at
"peace" with sin is the worst punishment of all, for
then the sinner is comatose.

The silence of God is broken and he speaks his words
in Sacred Scripture. As this word, like God himself,
lives across generations of people, the blood bond of
union extends also through the centuries, backward as
well as forward. For this reason, the Bible, which reflects God's intervention in history, seems to defy the
laws of chronological history. In the Bible, Moses or
David or Jeremiah is continuously alive, and their words
are always modulating in a living way to new times
and circumstances. In this context of one community
across generations, we find atonement by union, not
substitution.

Once sin is committed, evil is released across the
centuries, backward and forward. No one, even in the
past, can be fully at rest if anyone, even in the future,
is sick and sinful. The power of goodness, ejecting this
sin, comes from all directions. Hopes for the future
purify as much as nobility inherited from one's fore-

fathers. Later generations can repay for the gift of life (if that were ever possible) by atoning for the sins of their parents; present generations can sustain the hope that their children's children will correct the mistakes and sins of today!

From this consideration, we can conclude that sin always brings suffering somewhere across the centuries and that suffering always implies sin somewhere in the genealogical tree. Suffering must be qualified as the purifying force of goodness, ejecting evil.

The prayers of supplication in the Psalter bring to us the faith and perseverance of our forefathers, challenging our consciences to measure up to their goodness, sustaining us in our sorrows lest we lose faith. Such goodness from the past keeps us from becoming comatose and so induces more suffering in our personal lives as well as in our communities.

These ideas are related to a number of important theological questions, such as original sin, merit and indulgence, prayers of petition for others, the suffering souls in purgatory. These traditional expressions of faith will not be denied, but only enriched and expressed in contemporary terms if they are studied in the context of atonement by union (instead of substitution). This union embraces the centuries, continuing its bond of life even where death has taken place.

These general theological notions about prayer and suffering, life and death, will be exemplified in the second major part of this essay.

Part 2. The Living Context of Prayer

Up till now we have delayed over the religious formation of Israel regarding sin, suffering, and death.

We now listen with respect to our Israelite neighbors at prayer. As they reveal their soul in our presence, we will be ashamed and yet thankful for such a communication of spirit. We will first participate in a *community* recital of Psalm 12. Then we will share the whispered prayer of an *individual* worshiper in Psalms 22 and 69. Finally, we will weigh the stern and heavy asceticism of the "curse psalms."

The Community Supplication

Prayers of supplication in the Psalter can be divided into large sections: *individual* supplications with the use of the singular ("*My* God . . . why have you abandoned *me*?" (Ps 22) and *community* supplications in the plural ("O God, *our* ears have heard . . . Yet now you have cast *us* off" (Ps 44). We leave aside the extended discussion whether the singular "I" expresses the bond of unity and the one voice of all the community. A quick reply would be "Most probably yes!" Nonetheless, the individual supplications seem to have preserved traces of their "eremitical" origin and continue to reflect the solitude of the human heart. The community supplications, so it seems, do not reflect such personalized pathos. This loss is part of the cost paid by the psalmist, who had selflessly lost himself (or herself) totally within the people of God.

An outline of Psalm 12 will exemplify the larger structure and the community interaction of this type of prayer. We follow the versification of the Hebrew Bible.

(I)	V. 1	Title	Vague rubrical details
	V. 2a'	Introduction	"Save, O Lord!"—
			possibly repeated at

			different times during the psalm by the *entire* assembly
(II)	V. 2a''-9	Main Part	*Combines various styles* (lament, oracle, confidence) and *speakers* (at least two choral groups representing good and evil persons; individuals such as a cantor and a priest)
(a)	V. 2a''-5 V. 2a''-4	Lament	The words of "the poor." Are they a special class, known as the Hasidim or the Anawim? Possibly sung by a *cantor.*
	V. 5		Sung by a choral group, representing evil persons
(b)	V. 6	Oracle	Pronounced by a priest in the name of God, assuring relief.
(c)	VV. 7-9	Prayer of Confidence	Choral response of faith to the divine oracle

In this psalm two qualities of biblical spirituality come directly to our attention: (1) the realism of the

Bible and (2) the role of faith, sustaining one before God without providing definitive answers.

Realism—Consistency with Continuity

Very realistically, the psalm allows the wicked to speak for themselves. A special choral group is chosen to speak aloud the boastful libertarianism of the godless. Such a public proclamation at worship brings out a further aspect of biblical realism, this time rather embarrassingly, to the "pious ones" assembled for prayer. The wicked, we see from verse 2 onward, are members of a community who tend to destroy community by their insincerity, jealousy, and unreliability. They *use* community as a platform for their subjective harangues against the unifying members by restricting expectations of love. This crime is committed by all of us who at times make our contributions to a group so individualistic as to be destructive of any forceful unity or goal in that group!

This psalm, at the very beginning, deplores the end of the *hasid* and the sweeping away of the *'emunim* (these Hebrew words are translated "dutiful" and "faithful"). The root idea of *hasid* denotes a blood or family bond, the basis of the closely knit tribal structure of Israelite society.

This family unity or *hasid* ought to express itself spontaneously, in a clear and reliable way. Such an expectation is enunciated by the other Hebrew word, *'emunim*. It states to a Hebrew: *Be* what you are *supposed* to be because to who or what you really *are*. This word, *'emunim,* derives from a root, spoken many times a day across the world at prayer: *amen*. Thus two main characteristics of *amen* are (1) consistency, being truly and sincerely yourself in words and actions, and (2) continuity, remaining always dependable toward others through the years. Understandably, then, *amen* provides the principal Hebrew word for "faith," namely, the derivative *'emeth.*

Faith primarily describes an *interior* reality which gradually—at times explosively—but always surely transforms surface reality. Thus, through faith, a person's words and actions genuinely and perseveringly reveal his or her interior qualities, their *'enumin.* Moreover, because faith in God strengthened the natural bonds that fibered the Israelite tribal system, *faith* was also the principal cause of Israel's *hasid* or community.

The Faith to Wait

Realism, we say, characterized biblical faith; the Bible doesn't pretend things are different or better than they really are. Psalm 12 does not seem to get anywhere, and it can stand condemned, like religion in any age, because life goes on the same, with and without God. Psalm 12 ends where it started, for we are told in the last verse that "around about us wicked people still strut" and vaunt themselves! One can ask, Is prayer useless?

If prayer dictated a timetable of changes to God, it would indeed be worthless. Not only are God's plans far beyond man's—like the distance of the heavens over the earth, according to Psalms 103:11 and Isaiah 55:9 —but these plans embrace *all* men and cannot truly save one person unless that person is ready to bring his or her interior qualities, their *'enumin.* Moreover, because faith in God strengthened the natural bonds of love. Human prayer, to be genuine, must resonate the quality of a blood bond, where each human being receives, enjoys, and transmits life.

Very rightly, then, faith can appreciate the divine oracle in verse 6, which combines God's declaration, "Now I arise! I give salvation!" with his expectation to "wait for it!" The tension of life is to maintain a confidence that God is present as savior *now,* even though one must wait for his full revelation.

The seeming contradiction and the real tension of biblical faith show up here in still another way. The psalm opens with "*Save,* O Lord!" and the same Hebrew word recurs in the divine oracle of verse 6, "I give *salvation!*" Yet the psalm concludes in verse 9 with the wicked still ignoring God and shattering the joyful family bond of God's people. Yet the open-mindedness of "waiting" for what is "now" (according to verse 6) is implied in the subtle grammar of the introductory exclamation, "Save, O Lord!" This word, *save,* is a transitive verb, both in Hebrew and (normally) in English, and presumes an object to be saved. When the Hebrew psalm has no direct object, something is missing in the psychological nuance of the sentence. It implies "Wait . . . for only God can explain what this salvation will accomplish, for whom he will act, and when. Wait . . . till God finishes the sentence."

Psalm 12, then, a community lament, combines a sturdy faith with an embarrassing realism. Its style of prayer invites us to wait with the Bible at heart!

Supplication for the Individual

The other main type of prayer in the Book of Psalms —written in the singular, rather than the plural—is the supplication of an *individual.* This group of psalms manifests an even richer variety of mood and responses than the collective supplication. There are prayers of the aged (Ps 71), the sick (Pss 6, 31, 41, 88), the innocent under persecution (Pss 7, 17, 26), the penitent sinner (Pss 51 and 130). Within this large number of psalms can occur the curse of the enemy.

If one understands human nature, which is capable of cursing its opponents and, with God's grace, rising to beg forgiveness, then one cannot only accept but thoroughly appreciate the wide span of human emotions in the individual prayers of supplication. From these psalms one can develop a psychological response to anger, frustration, and sickness, as well as a theological synthesis of sin, compunction, and forgiveness. For our part, limitations of space restrict our discussion to Psalms 22 and 69 and to the problem of the curse psalms.

A Mystic Liturgical Response in Faith

Psalm 22 ranks among the gems of the Psalter, composed by a mystic who long contemplated the confessions of Jeremiah, the songs of the suffering servant in Second Isaiah, the penitential prayers of the Miserere (Ps 51), and the memoirs of Nehemiah. So rich is the tradition converging here that a scholar like Hans-Joachim Kraus claims that the psalm is the product of many authors over a long period of time! In the fullness of that time Jesus Christ consecrated Psalm 22 by his blood and dying breath. The opening words of the psalm were among his last, proclaimed from the pulpit of the cross. In Psalm 22 Jesus found the shelter of some understanding when he was abandoned by his

Father at the moment of death.

The author of Psalm 22 does not mention external details of his life. He hides beneath a rich symbolism and abandons himself to whatever a person will make of it! This sufferer makes no allusion to sin, nor any appeal to innocence. He does not smart under irritation or anger. He does not psychoanalyze himself or distract himself with philosophic preoccupation over the nature of human suffering. We find no sourness or bitterness. Simply, he abandons himself into the hands of a God who had abandoned him, and in this surrender he experiences the peace and hope of God's presence.

The mood of the psalmist modulates so spontaneously that we hardly notice any change:

Vv. 2-3	Invocation of God	V. 12	Prayer
Vv. 4-6	Motivation of faith	Vv. 13-19	Lament
Vv. 7-9	Lament	Vv. 20-22	Prayer
Vv. 10-11	Confidence	Vv. 23-27	Song of thanksgiving

(Verses 28-32 are another song of thanksgiving, definitely by a different author at a later time.)

The key word of the psalm seems to be the Hebrew equivalent for "distant" or "far away" (*rahoq*). In verse 2 it expresses the fact, or better a question about the fact: "My God! My God! Why have you abandoned me? *Far* from my salvation be the words of my cry!" In verses 12 and 20 the question modulates into a prayer: "Do not be *far away* from me." The non-mystic among us can put many questions to the psalmist. How can be say "My God" to the God who has abandoned him? How can such a God possibly hear him? In answer, the psalmist might say: One suffers abandonment only from a friend or a lover, never from a stranger. If love has ceased, abandonment is no longer *suffered*!

May we also add that "loss," in this case, is one of those examples where love has leapt so far beyond intellectual understanding, and even beyond consciousness, that the human person is "lost" within the ecstacy of God's embrace? On these same terms, only a mystic, experiencing profound prayer in God while searching for the absent God, is qualified to touch that most profound of theological mysteries: How could the man Jesus, in dying, know that he was God?

Because the psalmist took the traditions of his people very seriously and firmly believed in the presence and goodness of God, he had problems with his faith. If he had had the least doubt about God, he would already have had the answer to his question. If in moments of doubt he had lowered the standard of God's fidelity to that of man's—perhaps faithful but perhaps not—then this moment of loss and suffering was simply one of those "perhaps not" days of God. Because of this uncompromising faith, that God *is always faithful*, the psalmist became the mystic, swept beyond the statements of his faith to their deepest experience. The forward sweep of the mystic, be it noted, is an entirely different direction than the backward thrust of the doubter, who crashes against his own faith.

Presence within Community . . . Becomes Jesus

The French scholar, Father Albert Gelin, recognized four main stages in the interpretation of this psalm. His final words were dictated as he lay dying of cancer and were posthumously published in *The Psalms Are Our Prayer* (Liturgical Press, Collegeville, Minn.). This and another small book, *The Poor of Yahweh,* summarize Gelin's position on the history of Psalm 22.

The author belonged to the *Anawin.* (Against a more common opinion, Gelin understood these persons to constitute a separate religious sect within Israel, like the later Pharisees and Zealots.) Unjustly imprisoned and stricken with serious illness, the psalmist contemplated the Holy Scriptures, and gradually a poem took shape in his heart which was to become a world classic. Verses 2-27 came to birth. The *second stage* arrived when the psalm forced its way into public prayer by the sheer power of its mystic beauty. A private person's prayer now expresses the thoughts of a community. The popularity of the psalm for sustaining the hopes of the community enabled it to become a carrier of messianic faith for the future.

The *third stage* developed as the psalm absorbed the community's later reflections upon suffering and bodily resurrection. Verses 28-32 were added at this later time. Finally, the *fourth stage,* of rereading and reinterpreting the psalm, arrived when New Testament writers felt that in this psalm God provided them with an excellent means to contemplate the mystery of Jesus. Jesus must have first given them the example.

From the viewpoint of prophecy fulfillment, this long tradition of Psalm 22 indicated that Jesus did not so much match up to word predictions as relive the full gamut of Israel's experiences and hopes over the centuries. By uniting himself to them, Jesus purified and consecrated them most fully to God.

In verses 23-27, we see that a liturgical action accompanied Psalm 22 and was incorporated within its words. Reference is made to a sacrificial banquet of thanksgiving for the community of the *Anawim* or "the poor." This "sacrifice" receives its meaning from the words and actions of the psalmist. Just as his faith precipitated his problem, his words will sharpen the trials and intensify the suffering of the community. Recall that the psalmist *suffered* the problem of hopes, stirred by his exceptional faith. It is possible, we think, to transfer these same elements of interaction of individual and community, through liturgical sacrifice, to the sacrifice of Jesus on the cross and its reliving within the liturgical sacrifice of the Mass.

The Cleansing of God's House

Along with Psalm 22, Psalm 69 ranks as one of the major biblical sources for the New Testament theology about Jesus' death and resurrection. We restrict our remarks to verse 10, "Zeal for your house consumes me." In John's gospel, this line was cited at the cleansing of the temple. His disciples are said to recall the words of the psalm after witnessing Jesus' angry reaction against the money changers. The gospel account then continues:

> At this the Jews responded, "What sign can you show us authorizing you to do these things?" "Destroy this temple," was Jesus' answer, "and in three days I will raise it up." They retorted. "This temple took forty-six years to build, and you are going to 'raise it up in three days'?" Actually he was talking about the temple of his body. Only after Jesus had been raised from the dead did his disciples recall that he had said this and come to believe the Scripture and the word he had spoken. (John 2:18-22)

If we compare John's gospel with the psalm, "house" or "temple" modulates with a variety of meanings. (1) In Psalm 69, "house" refers to the *people Israel* among whom God dwelt, yet who were opposing the psalmist in his zeal for their conversion. (2) In John's gospel, there is a shift of meaning, because "house" now clearly refers not to the people Israel but to the *Jerusalem sanctuary*. (3) Yet this place of worship suddenly becomes symbolic of *Jesus himself* in his reference to his passion and resurrection: "He was talking about the temple of his body." (4) Because of the liturgical context of John's gospel, we might also see an extension to Jesus' *eucharistic presence* within the Church today.

It may be helpful to present these four different nuances schematically beneath the key words of the psalm: *zeal, house, consumes.*

Zeal for your	*house*	*consumes me.*
(1) Goodness of the psalmist	The sinful people Israel	Personal suffering endured by the psalmist
(2) Goodness of Jesus during his ministry	The profaned Jerusalem temple	Suffering endured by those profaning the Jerusalem temple
(3) Goodness of Jesus in his passion-resurrection	Sinful men and women	Jesus' personal suffering on the cross
(4) Goodness of Jesus in the Church and Eucharist	Our sins today, profaning the Church	Our personal sufferings from the purifying of Jesus' presence

In all cases the cause of suffering is the presence of goodness within a wicked "house." Earlier in this essay, we mentioned that a strong body (typical of goodness) always suffers its diseases more than a weakened, debilitated body; and the latter can easily lapse into a coma.

The words of the psalm not only become ever more personal and interior, but they converge and unite. "Zeal," "house," and "consumes" symbolize actions within Jesus himself. On the cross he *is* the temple infested with sin, through the world to which he has united himself. This "temple" of his body is cleansed and literally consumed by violence. Jesus is also the zeal and goodness of God. The zeal which charged against evil (in the Jerusalem temple) and destroyed his own body in death (on the cross) was also the power obedient to God for raising this temple back to life in the resurrection.

The eucharistic presence of Jesus is symbolic of the Church. This Church is sinful; this temple is profaned. The presence of Jesus' charity inflicts severe suffering, for it cannot tolerate a divided and sinful Church. This pain purifies and strengthens. Divine hopes seem at times to destroy the Church, yet in this obedience the Church rises to new life. This union of Jesus, as he hung on the cross and as he resides within the Church, explains the oneness of the sacrifice of the cross and its continuation, realistically, in the Church and liturgically in the Eucharist.

The Curse Psalms

Many reasons converge for maintaining the curse psalms within Christian liturgical prayer. Admittedly, none of them is sufficient in isolation from the others, but together they might build a dam strong enough to hold back the floodwater of opinion against these psalms. The following evidence summarizes an article of this writer in *The Bible Today:* "Does the Bible Preach Hate?" (Feb. 1970).

(a) To clear away the misunderstanding that the curse psalms might belong to the "hate" or "injustice" theology of the ages before Christ, we draw attention to the New Testament, which continues the same tradition. We can refer to Jesus' action in cleansing the temple; his words to hate father, mother, wife, etc. (Luke 14:26); his condemnation of the Pharisees (Matt 23); or the cry of the persecuted saints in Revelation 16:5-6 that their tormentors be forced to drink their own blood, thus "getting what they deserve." Even the gentle Mary, in her Magnificat, announces that God will depose the mighty and send the rich away empty (Luke 2:52-53).

(b) *Semitic exaggeration.* Semites cannot curse in four-letter words, only in paragraphs which lash out against parents, spouses, children, relatives, descendants, etc., etc. While speaking of Oriental style, we must remark that in the line in Psalm 137:9, about "smashing your little ones against the rock," expresses a wish *in Oriental style* that the city walls of Babylon ("the rock") be beaten to the ground and their defenders ("little ones") be conquered.

(c) *Events* at times are *narrated* in the Bible simply *because they happened.* The Scriptures do not necessarily approve of all that takes place, and they leave the reader to his own thinking! At other times the juxtaposition of events tells its own story and shouts louder than words, exempli gratia, Genesis 37 about the moral courage of Joseph and Genesis 38 about the easy immorality of Judah!

Today, if we were to read in church a scene of violence from the Bible and see the horrified faces of the congregation, we have only to stop and quietly ask, Are we just as startled by the violence we ourselves inflict at times upon one another—in our slums, in our prisons, in our family quarrels, in our international wars?

(d) Biblical spirituality does not remove *the sad effects of sin*. Violence begets violence; sin brings suffering. Only thus can the poison be ejected by a strong body. As mentioned, a strong body suffers even more violently the effects of poisoning in its system than does a weak body. In forgiving sin, God seldom if ever takes away this suffering consequence of sin; the image of Jesus on his cross burns this fact into our minds.

(e) The Bible makes no theoretical distinction, such as "hate sin but love the sinner." Sin does not exist unless in the sinner. Do evil thoughts exist independently of evil minds? Can the hand kill, once it is cut off from the killer? Is the hand a murderer, or the person who possesses the hand? What is more, can the killer be redeemed if he never realizes that he did anything wrong? And can he learn the full meaning of evil without experiencing its agony?

(f) Some persons have no other prayer but the curse psalms—such as the Jews in Nazi concentration camps; social and racial outcasts who see no chance even for their babies to escape the slums; prisoners dehumanized by the personal outrages to which even fellow prisoners subject them. In fact, these persons may have been so dehumanized by brutality that they can no longer muster enough strength to pray—not even to pray a psalm of hate. Someone must pray in their place and cry out the violence of their outrage. Someone must thunder God's hateful wrath at the sight of such barbarity against his loved ones. Can the liturgy of our churches ignore these people and offer no voice to these muted persons who have only one kind of prayer?

(g) No nation in recorded history has suffered more than the Jewish people. Their history is seared and slashed—from their enslavement in Egypt in the thirteenth century before Christ to the Nazi pogroms in the twentieth century after Christ. Those who uttered the curse psalms against their enemies were themselves the victims of this violent purification.

Perhaps the fear of the curse psalms stems today from an unspoken dread, deep within the subconscious mind of the Christian, that to curse evil is like making a vow to suffer. God takes those promises seriously. No one is without sin. The curse against evil will boomerang, as it did for Israel.

We who are sinners need the hate of the Bible so that the violence of sin will not destroy us but rather be recognized as a means of resurrecting us from moral death, a new people of God, whose greatest purity lies in our total love for the neighbor.

Conclusion

It may seem strange, even an outrage against the biblical injunction to meekness in Psalm 37:11, to conclude this essay with the violent language of the curse psalms. We might also ask how the Book of Isaiah, with its Immanuel prophecy in chapter 7 and its command to "comfort, oh, comfort my people" in chapter 40, could possibly end with the horrifying scene of rotting corpses outside the heavenly Jerusalem (Is 66:24). Yet the gospels present the ministry of Jesus as concluding with his own terrifying eschatological discourses, and the last book of the New Testament also describes in violent terms the war between goodness and evil.

If the curse psalms shock us into silence, the hymns of praise violently sweep us beyond words into exstasy and the prayers of supplication extend us like a taut rope between the poles of "My God" and "abandonment" (Ps 22:2).

The psalms reflect the moment of *faith,* when God invades the *realism* of his people's lives with the echilarating demands of hope and goodness. This moment can absorb a person into speechless wonder; it can also cast him into throes of suffering. It can even combine these irreconcilable emotions, as John and Paul of the Cross confessed.

The community consciousness of the psalms declares that no person can long be at peace in separation from those with whom he or she forms one bond of blood. Here is the realism of God's charity among his people. The psalms, therefore, in their history move back and forth between the individual and the community. The individual finds God in the experience of the community, the Church, or the cosmos; these cannot be separated. The discovery of God in fellow human beings induces the mystic contemplation of God in himself. As one ponders this mystery of God, one returns to the community, articulating hopes and holiness that up till now were beyond the dreams and courage of everyone. To pray the psalms, one must be rooted in the experience of community and lost in wonder with the experience of God.

The psalms mean praying from *this kind* of reality, where the most radical differences unite: abandonment with union, loss with gain. The mystic who suffers the abandonment of faith is joyfully consoled by the words of Jesus: Whoever loses his life for my sake is saving it (Luke 9:24).

The Death of God's Son
and the
Beginning of the New Age

Donald Senior C.P.
Catholic Theological Union
Chicago, Illinois

REDACTION criticism, that branch of biblical studies which focuses on the composition of the gospels, reveals that the evangelists were not merely reporters or custodians of the Church's archives. They were creative authors, who not only handed on traditions about the life of Jesus but helped shape and reinterpret those traditions to form a coherent literary whole.

Such a description of "evangelist" certainly fits Matthew. His adaptation of the Gospel of Mark and of the collection of the sayings of Jesus, commonly called "Q," achieved a masterful restatement of the gospel story. However, a first reading of Matthew's passion narrative (chaps. 26 and 27 of the gospel) gives the impression that the evangelist's creativity is less in evidence here than, for example, in earlier chapters of the gospel, such as the Sermon on the Mount or the miracle collection of chapters 8 and 9. In the passion narrative, Matthew rigorously follows the order of scenes presented by Mark, and even the verse-by-verse identity is greater in these two chapters than in any other portion of the gospel.

This homogeneity between Matthew and Mark in the passion account is due in part to the fact that the passion story was knitted together early in the community's history and has an inner coherence which discourages extensive rearrangement or adaptation. In fact, all four evangelists show substantial agreement in the passion story (at least from the arrest scene on). But a careful reading of the passion account reveals that, even here, Matthew has not abandoned his role of creatively interpreting the gospel tradition.[1] Before focusing on one aspect of this interpretation, let us catalogue some of the distinctive features of Matthew's presentation in chapters 26 and 27.

Many of the changes Matthew introduces are simply stylistic. As he has done throughout the gospel, the evangelist freely recasts Mark's material into a generally improved Greek style. Where Mark is often abrupt and repetitive, Matthew consistently introduces order and coherence. But not all of Matthew's alterations are aesthetic. A careful sifting of the changes often reveals a new or different perspective that distinguishes Matthew from Mark. The light of the community's faith in Jesus as the Risen Lord breaks more noticeably into the darkness of the passion in Matthew than in Mark. Jesus demonstrates his mastery of the situation by prophetic knowledge of what is to take place (26:2, 18). He is well aware of who will betray him (26:25) and anticipates Judas' fateful kiss (26:50). If he wishes, he could invoke the aid of legions of angels (26:53), and his power is sufficient to destroy even the temple (26:61). Christological titles such as "Lord" (26:22), "Christ" (26:68; 27:17, 22), and "Son of God" (27:40, 43) are added to enrich the text.

Many of Matthew's alterations echo themes that are developed throughout the gospel. Thus the stress on Jesus' obedience in Gethsemane and in the arrest scene is consistent with a fundamental perspective that is evident from the opening chapters of the gospel (cf. Matt 3:15, 5:17ff., 6:10). A concern with Israel's rejection of the gospel and its subsequent proclamation to the gen-

tiles (cf. 8:10, 22:43) emerges in special Matthean passion scenes such as the death of Judas in 27:3-10 and
the climax of the trial scene in 27:24-25. The Sermon
on the Mount's prohibition against the use of violence
is affirmed in Jesus' admonition at the moment of his
arrest (26:52). Matthew's aversion to taking oaths
(5:33-37) is further illustrated in the tragedy of Peter's
sworn denial of his master (26:72, 74). And Matthew's
distinctive emphasis on the fulfillment of Scripture, a
note sounded through his gospel, continues with such
texts as 26:54, 56 and 27:9-10.

In all of these examples, Matthew has added to or
significantly altered the text of his source in order to
make his point. Such illustrations of the evangelist at
work could be multiplied. However, within the scope
of this chapter, we would like to settle on one intriguing scene of the passion story where the evangelist
shows particular care and creativity in his adaptation
of his source. In 27:51-54, immediately following the
death of Jesus, Matthew adds a series of amazing
"signs" to Mark's report of the tearing of the temple
veil. It is to an interpretation of these signs and their
significance within the overall gospel message of Matthew that we now turn.

The Setting (Matt 27:32-56)

Spectacular events are triggered by Jesus' death: the
veil of the temple is split in two from top to bottom,
the earth quakes, the rocks are split, tombs are opened,
and the bodies of "the saints" are raised up and (after
Jesus' resurrection) appear to many in Jerusalem. These
extraordinary happenings are fitted into the final scene
of the passion story: the crucifixion and death of Jesus

(Matt 27:32-56). Before examining the signs in detail, we should give some attention to this larger context.

As is true of the entire passion narrative, Matthew records the sequence of events exactly as in Mark, that is, the way of the cross (v. 32), offering of a drink of wine and gall (vv.33f.), crucifixion of Jesus and division of his garments (v. 35), emplacement of the placard indicating the charge (v. 37), crucifixion of two thieves (v. 38), mockery by the passersby and the two thieves (vv. 39-44), darkness (v. 45), Jesus' citation of Psalms 22:2 (vv. 45-46), reaction of the bystanders (vv. 47-49), death of Jesus (v. 50), resulting signs (vv. 51-53), confession of the centurion (v. 54), and the presence of the faithful women (vv. 55-56).

Within this framework, however, Matthew introduces a number of changes. Some can be left out of consideration, either because they are of a purely stylistic variety or have only limited importance for Matthew's interpretation of the scene. In the latter category might be included Matthew's addition of the phrase "mixed with gall" (cf. 27:34), which highlights the allusion to Psalm 69:22; his mention of the watchful presence of the guard next to the cross (27:36); and the clarification of the action when Jesus' appeal to the Father (v. 46) is misunderstood as a calling of Elias. (In Mark, the *same* man who runs to get the wine-soaked sponge is the one who prevents the offering [cf. Mark 15:36].) In Matthew, one of the crowd (v. 48) goes for the wine but "the others" (v. 49) prevent him from offering it to Jesus.

But other changes are more significant, and their accumulation indicates the thrust of Matthew's interpretation. Primary among these is Matthew's fortification of the mockery scene. In Mark's presentation (15:

29–32) the mockers' insults recall the accusations in the
trial before the Sanhedrin (cf. 14:58–62). The crucified
Jesus is taunted for his alleged threats against the temple (15:29) and for his claim to be the Christ (15:32).
His miraculous descent from the cross is the sign de-
manded for faith ("that we might see"), a request that
recalls the Pharisees' demand for a sign in Mark 8:11–
13.

Matthew absorbs the basic content of Mark but includes some notable additions. The taunts of the passersby (Matt 27:40) are fortified by the phrase "if you are
the Son of God," a phrase that evokes Wisdom 2:18
and the wider context of Psalm 22. (We will return to
these sources shortly.) A more immediate allusion is to
the temptation scene in chapter 4 of Matthew's gospel.
Satan prefaces the first two temptations with the identical protasis: "if you are the Son of God" (cf. Matt
4:3, 6). The evangelist thus seems to suggest that the
mockers continue the work of Satan. They are "test-
ing" the fidelity of God's Son by attempting to deter
the Messiah from the path of obedience he has chosen.

The most important addition is found in verse 43.
These words of the mockers have no parallel in Mark's
account: "He relied on God; let God rescue him now
if he wants to. After all, he claimed, 'I am God's
Son.' " The verse is basically a citation of Psalm 22,
verse 9: "He relied on the Lord; let him rescue him,
if he loves him." Matthew's Greek text in this case
is neither identical with any form of the Septuagint we
know of nor is it a literal translation of the Hebrew
text. It would appear that in quoting the text he may
also have had in mind a similar passage from Wisdom
2:18. The author of Wisdom quotes this very verse of
Psalm 22 in his discussion of the sufferings of the just

man. We might also note that Matthew seems to add the last part of the verse: "After all, he claimed, 'I am God's Son'" (27:43b). These words underline the irony of the mockery. The Christian reader is well aware that Jesus *is* precisely what the bystanders blindly chide him for claiming to be.

The crucial point for our discussion is not what type of text Matthew may have appealed to (or more likely adapted) but what the significance of such an appeal to Psalm 22 and Wisdom 2 might be. Both of these Old Testament passages express the general theme of the "suffering just man." The just man trusts in Yahweh's faithfulness; he is a true "son of God." But his enemies and persecutors mock and torment him. They deride his claim to divine protection. Yahweh, however, is faithful, and the just man's sufferings are vindicated. We will return to a consideration of this theme of suffering and vindication when we have completed our survey of the context of 27:51-53.

In addition to his work on the mockery scene, Matthew makes some subtle alterations in the death scene itself. As in Mark's account, Jesus' dying words are a citation of Psalm 22 (Mark 15:34; Matt 27:46). The verse is quoted first in Aramaic, an archaism that testifies to an early use of this psalm in the passion tradition.[2] As we will note below, the opening words of the psalm on Jesus' lips signal the fundamental interpretation that the community and the evangelists give to the death of Jesus.

The words of Jesus (*eli, eli,* "my God, my God") are either misunderstood or deliberately misinterpreted as a call for Elijah. Jewish piety often invoked this Old Testament prophet in times of crisis. And in late Judaism, as well as in the New Testament itself, the

coming of Elijah has been associated with the dawn of
messianic times. Whatever his motivation, one of the
bystanders recognizes that Jesus is near death and runs
to obtain some wine for the dying "criminal." But
the rest (at least as Matthew conceives the sequence)
prevent this act of consideration and taunt Jesus once
more, saying, "Let us see whether Elijah comes to his
rescue" (27:49).

The death of Jesus follows immediately. In Mark,
Jesus emits a "loud cry" and expires (15:37). Commentators have been baffled by this wordless shout. Is
it a cry of agony? Or of victory? Or is it somehow
connected with the exorcism theme of the gospel? Since
the evangelist has not provided any hint to his meaning, interpretation is difficult. Matthew, however, is
more helpful. The last cry of Jesus is not spelled out,
but subtle changes in the verse clearly indicate how
Matthew interprets this final moment of Jesus' life
(27:50).

First of all, Matthew inserts the word *palin* ("again"),
thereby explicitly relating Jesus' utterance in verse 50
to the citation of Psalm 22:2 in verse 46. Matthew also
substitutes the work *kraxas* (to "cry out") for Mark's
apheis (to "emit"). Although the verb *krazo* is a common Greek word and its use here should not be over-
interpreted, it is interesting to note that the same verb
is used in the Greek version of Psalm 22 to describe
the desperate cries of the just man to Yahweh (cf. Ps
22:3, 5, 24). Finally, Matthew uses the expression
"gave up his spirit," rather than Mark's "expired,"
to describe Jesus' death. It is generally conceded that
Matthew's rendition emphasizes more clearly than
Mark's the voluntary nature of Jesus' death. God's Son
obediently yields up the spirit of life to his Father. This

Thus Jesus' claim to be God's Son, and the vindication of that claim, become a central focus of Matthew's passion narrative. The title "Son of God" is, of course, not limited to the death scene. It occurs nine times in the gospel. Two of these occurrences are in the temptation scene, where, as we have noted, Satan prefaces the first two tests of Jesus with "If you are the Son of God" (cf. Matt 4:3, 5). The title is found again on the lips of demonic spirits in 8:29, when the Gadarene devils futilely attempt to prevent their exorcism interpretation is explicitly developed by Luke, in whose account Jesus dies while praying the words of Psalm 31:6: "Father, into your hands I commend my spirit" (Luke 23:46).

This survey of Matthew's changes in the scenes immediately preceeding the eruption of the extraordinary signs (27:51-53) helps us understand the evangelist's perspective. Emphasis falls on Jesus' claim to be the "Son of God." In 27:40 the "tempters" preface their taunts with the phrase "if you are God's Son." In 27:43 an explicit allusion to Wisdom 2:18, and ultimately to Psalm 22:9, again focuses on this claim of Jesus. The placement of Psalm 22:1 on the dying lips of Jesus (27:46, 50) repeats the thematic. Jesus prays as the just man, as the believer who claims God's protection and vindication because he trusts his Father. The citation of the first verse of the psalm should not be limited to an enigmatic cry of despair. The overall context, and in both cases the title is added by Matthew. In 14:33 the disciples respond to Jesus' walking on the water with a formal confession of faith: "Beyond doubt, you are the Son of God." As we shall magnificent vindication of that faith, brought about by a trustworthy God.

by invoking Jesus' name. Two other passages in the earlier chapters of the gospel are in a confessional context and in both cases the title is added by Matthew. In 14:33 the disciples respond to Jesus' walking on the water with a formal confession of faith: "Beyond doubt, you are the Son of God." As we shall see, this passage is evoked at the end of the death scene in Matthew 27:54, when the centurion and his companions proclaim Jesus in exactly the same words. And finally, in 16:16, Peter announces: "You are the Messiah, the Son of the Living God" (a confession that is much more emphatic than the parallel in Mark [cf. 8:29]).

The four remaining occurrences of the title are in the passion narrative itself, as we have noted. The decided confessional context of most of the Son-of-God texts shows the importance of this designation for Matthew's Christology. But the evangelist's identification of Jesus as "Son of God" cannot be limited to the explicit use of the title itself. Jesus' designation of God as "my Father" is a peculiar characteristic of Matthew's gospel (cf. 7:21, 10:32f., 12:50, 15:13, 16:17, 18:10, 19:35, 20:23, 25:34, 26:53). And it is obvious that this emphasis is closely aligned with a predilection for the "Son of God" title. In Matthew 26:29, for example, Mark's phrase "in the kingdom of God" (14:25) is altered to read "in the kingdom of *my Father*." In the Gethsemane scene, the obedience of Jesus as Son is stressed by his repeated prayer to the Father (26:39, 42). The second prayer (26:42) clearly alludes to the Lord's prayer of 6:9f., with its obvious emphasis on filial obedience.

Further on in the passion account, the key question of the high priest at the trial becomes: "Are you the

Christ, the *Son of God*?"—the latter phrase a substitution for Mark's circumlocution, "Son of the Blessed
One?" (Mark 14:61). The high priest's question shows
that in the gospel, as in much of intertestamental
Judaism, the titles "Messiah" and "Son of God" become practically identical in designation. Thus Jesus'
claim to be the Christ, the Son of God, hangs in the
balance. He has appealed for God's vindication. He
dies in trustful obedience to his Father's will. The
scene is not set for the vindication of that messianic
obedience.

The Meaning of the Signs (Matt 27:51-53)

The vindication of Jesus as the Son of God, the issue
raised by Matthew's presentation of the death of Jesus,
is signified by the extraordinary events immediately following the obedient handing over of his spirit. Let us
examine each of these signs in turn and then attempt
to weave a coherent interpretation.

The Temple Veil

In both Mark and Matthew, the immediate result of
Jesus' death is a rending of the temple veil (cf. Mark
15:38, Matt 27:51a). The precise meaning of this sign
is not easily determined. Most commentators believe
that the veil referred to was the covering of the Holy
of Holies, the sacred inner sanctuary of the temple.
Others suggest it was the great veil that covered the
front of the temple itself.[3] The question cannot be decided with certitude, and, in any case, the evangelists
present this event not on the level of historical fact but
as a theological portent.

In *Mark's* case the sign seems to be negative in meaning. It is the climax of a critique against the temple that erupts in such passages as 11:11ff., 12:33, 13:2, etc. At a climactic moment of the trial, Jesus is accused of dire threats against the Jerusalem temple, "made by hands," and of stating that after three days he would raise up a temple "not made by hands" (cf. 14:58). Thus Jesus' death signifies the end of the temple economy and the beginning of the new worshiping community, represented by the confession of the gentile centurion (15:30).

But *Matthew's* addition of other portents, besides the tearing of the veil, may give a more positive nuance to his presentation. The tearing of the veil is no longer in neat polarity with the messianic confession of the centurion. It is the first of a *series* of signs (earthquake, rending of rocks, opening of tombs) that lead to the most spectacular result of Jesus' death, the raising of the saints. Thus the tearing of the veil seems to be an *opening*—the beginning of a new way to life and salvation. The veil before the Holy of Holies not only signified the locus of God's presence at the heart of Israel's cultic life but served as a wall of separation between the people and Yahweh, the "wholly other."

This symbolism of a "new beginning" echoes other New Testament texts, such as Hebrews 6:19-20 and 10:19-20, which speak of Jesus' salvific death in terms of his opening a way into the sanctuary. Thus Matthew, at least, may be implying that the tearing of the temple veil signifies not only the end of the temple economy but the beginning of a new age. As we shall see, the symbolism of the additional signs tends to support this interpretation.

The Earthquake, the Splitting of the Rocks, the Opening of the Tombs (Matt 27:52)

The signs move in measured rhythm toward their climax, the resurrection of the saints. All of the passive verbs are closely linked: the veil was *torn* in two and the earth *quaked* and the rocks *split* and the tombs *opened*. Thus the earthquake and the splitting of the rocks are intermediary events leading to Matthew's main point of interest.

As is often the case where Matthew chooses to develop some portion of the gospel story, he draws his imagery from the Old Testament. A tremor of the earth is part of the imagery traditionally associated with a manifestation of Yahweh's power in the Old Testament. The Canticle of Deborah, for example, associates this sign with Yahweh's saving acts in the exodus:

> O Lord, when you sent out from Seir, when you marched from the land of Edom, the earth quaked and the heavens were shaken, while the clouds sent down showers. Mountains trembled in the presence of the Lord, the One of Sinai, in the presence of the Lord, the God of Israel. (Judges 5:4–5).

Many prophetic texts reflect the same use of earthquake imagery with eschatological motifs (cf., e.g., Is 13:13, 24:18; Ez 38:19f.). Later writings, such as I Enoch 102:2, IV Ezra 9:2f., and II Baruch 32:1, continue the same theme. In the New Testament itself, texts such as Mark 13:8 (par. Matt 24:7) and the Book of Revelation (6:12, 8:5, 11:13, 19, 16:18) also exploit this image in apocalyptic descriptions of the coming judgment.

Thus the earthquake in Matt 27:52 is part of a sys-

tem of imagery that connotes the eschatological significance of Jesus' death. The final age seems to be
dawning. We have already remarked that the *function*
of the quake, besides its evocative power, is to lead
to the opening of the tombs—the climax of the eschatological signs. As such, the placement of the signs
strongly recalls the text of Ezekiel 37:7, where a tremor
of the earth precedes the revivification of the dry bones
in the prophet's great vision. Here, as in Matthew,
the earthquake is tied to a resurrection motif. As we
shall see, this passage is of prime importance for Matthew's interpretation of the death of Jesus.

The splitting of the rocks fits obviously into this
same framework. Functionally, it is a result of the
earthquake that will lead to the opening of the tombs.
Symbolically, it takes its place alongside the earthquake as part of the biblical symbolism that is used
to describe the manifestation of God's ultimate power
(cf. Nahum 1:5-6, I Kings 19:11, Ps 114:7f., Is 48:21).

The last link in the chain of events leading from the
death of Jesus to the resurrection of the saints is the
opening of the tombs. Obviously, the earthquake and
the splitting of the rocks are preparatory for the opening of the stone sepulchers. The vicinity of Jerusalem
was well known for this type of burial vault, chiseled
in the rock. But, once again, Matthew's interest is not
topographical. The intersection of Matthew's interpretive
presentation with chapter 37 of Ezekiel is repeated:

> Therefore, prophesy and say to them: Thus says the Lord
> God: O my people, I will open your graves and have you
> rise from them and bring you back to the land of Israel.
> Then you shall know that I am the Lord, when I open your
> graves and have you rise from them, O my people! (Ezekiel
> 37:12-13)

The Resurrection of the Saints (Matt 27:53)

The most spectacular sign resulting from the death of Jesus is recorded in 27:53: "Many bodies of saints who had fallen asleep were raised. After Jesus' resurrection, they came forth from their tombs and entered the holy city and appeared to many."

A host of interpretive problems surrounds this text, and our discussion cannot do full justice to their complexity.[4] But some general observations about the text can be helpful for understanding Matthew's intent. First of all, it is obvious that Matthew is not merely reporting a bizarre event that happened at the moment of Jesus' death. The general character of the signs and the complex chronology indicate that this sign, like the others, is to be understood as a theological statement about the meaning of the death of Jesus (i.e., the appearance of the saints must wait until after Jesus' resurrection, clearly indicating the primacy of the Lord's resurrection!).

Once again, the placement of this sign in the wider context of Jewish and biblical tradition provides leads to Matthew's meaning. In Daniel 12:2, perhaps the earliest biblical text referring to personal resurrection, we find a passage that has arresting similarities to Matthew 27:53: "Many of those who sleep in the dust of the earth shall awake." Numerous other passages in the intertestamental writings link a raising of the saints with God's victory over death in the final age (cf., e.g., I Enoch 49:3, II Baruch 11:4, Jubilees 23:1, IV Ezra 7:32, etc.). I Enoch 51:1 connects the liberation of the holy ones, trapped in Sheol, with the coming of the messianic age:

And in those days shall the earth also give back that which

has been entrusted to it, and Sheol also shall give back that
which it has received, and hell shall give back that which
it owes. For in those days, the Elect One shall arise, and
he shall choose the righteous and holy from among them,
for the day has drawn nigh that they should be saved.[5]

An even earlier text, Psalm 22, seems to link the
vindication of the just man, God's son, with the rescue
of the dead who are trapped in Sheol:

> To him alone shall bow down all who sleep in
>   the earth;
> Before him shall bend all who go down into the
>   dust. (Ps 22:30)

As we noted above, this Old Testament hymn, with
its theme of suffering and vindication, was of fundamental importance for the early Christian interpretation of the death of Jesus.

Thus the "saints" or "holy ones" referred to here
are obviously not the Christian saints (although the
Greek word *hagioi* refers to members of the community in Acts and Paul) but those leaders, prophets, and
martyrs of Israel who now "sleep" in death and whose
fidelity will be vindicated with the dawning of the new
age. The death of Jesus marks the beginning of this
decisive phase in salvific history, and the appearance
of the now revivified saints in Jerusalem (the capital
city, where popular tradition expected the general
resurrection to occur) testified to this marvel. Once
again, a parallel to the epic vision of Ezekiel 37 can
be noted. The vast army whose dried bones are sin-
ewed together and given living flesh are now able to
march back to Israel (37:12) that all may know the
power of Yahweh (37:13-14).

At several points in our discussion of Matt 27:51-53
we have noted possible allusions to Ezekiel's vision of

the dry bones. The vision's references to such things as an earthquake (37:7), the opening of the tombs (37:12, 13), the "spirit of life" (37:5-10, 14; cf. Matt 27:50), and the testimonial of the newly risen people (37:13-14) represent a convergence of elements which make allusion to this well-known Old Testament passage undeniable. The magnificent imagery of the dry bones vision helps us synthesize Matthew's presentation of the death scene. The original sense of the Ezekiel passage was to express a hope in the renewal of Israel after the tragedy of the exile. Although all hope seemed exhausted, the power of Yahweh raised up fresh life from a desert of bleached bones. Israel was not to die. Understandably, this text was soon applied to Israel's hopes for the messianic era. Rabbinic commentaries understood it as a prophecy of the general resurrection in the final age. The passage took its place in the cycle of Passover readings under this heading.[6]

There is other intriguing evidence of the text's function as an eschatological vision of hope. Chapter 37 of Exekiel is one of the passages on the scrolls that were buried in the floor of their synagogue by the Zealot defenders of Masada. There is no doubt that this scroll is to be dated prior to A.D. 73[7]. One can imagine what the vision of the dry bones must have meant to those apocalyptic warriors who were forced to watch helplessly as the Roman war machine made its irreversible progress toward the destruction of the Zealot fortress.

Another example of the vision's power as an expression of eschatological hope is found in the synagogue of Dura-Europos. One of the famous frescoes depicts the vision of Ezekiel with a convergence of imagery that has amazing similarity to Matthew 27:51-53. In a graphic presentation of the resuscitation of the dry bones, one finds evidence of an earthquake (a fissure in a mountain [the Mount of Olives?] and a crumbled house), figures who probably represent the risen saints proceeding toward Jerusalem, and, presiding over the entire scene, a powerful messianic figure who sends the spirits of life toward the dead saints.[8]

Thus Matthew's extraordinary signs are not extraordinary because their imagery is without parallel; they are extraordinary because the evangelist boldly asserts through them that the death of Jesus has inaugurated the final age. The eschatological hopes for God's vindication of Israel are fulfilled in the death of Jesus, God's Son.

This affirmation is punctuated by the centurion's confession (27:54). In Mark's account, the gentile soldier's acclamation of Jesus as the Son of God contrasts with the judgmental image of the tearing of the temple veil. In the dark hour of Jesus' death, the centurion is able accomplish what no one else in Mark's gospel was capable of doing: recognizing Jesus for who he is. Thus the death of Jesus has opened the way to the new worshiping community.

But in Matthew's account, this is no longer a singular dramatic confession. Jesus has already been recognized as Son of God by the disciples in the course of his public ministry (cf. Matt 14:33). The confession triggered by the marvelous signs at Jesus' death is also communitarian (cf. 27:54, the centurion *and those with him*). The cry of a single believer has become a chorus of faith. Jesus is the eschatological Lord, the Messiah whose death brings God's power breaking into human history.

The Death of Jesus and the Beginning of the New Age

Matthew's death scenario is complete. Jesus' claim to be God's Son is vindicated by the awesome events that follow his death. The new age has dawned, and the power of God reaches even into the abode of the dead, so that God's holy ones may taste the victory of resurrection. Jesus' prediction of the imminence of the final hour (26:18) is fulfilled, the *kairos* has come. Thus Matthew, as he has done throughout the gospel, gives historic significance to the life and death of Jesus. His ministry signaled the dawn of salvation for the people caught in darkness and misery (4:15-17). His teaching and mighty works were destined to bring to completion God's law and plan of salvation (5:17ff.). The ministry of his disciples announces the coming of the kingdom (10:7). The victory of God's Son in death and resurrection confirms the promise of the gospel: the kingdom has come!

But what, we might well ask, did such a statement mean for a community such as Matthew's? What did an assertion that the final age has dawned say to a community that suffered division (chaps. 18, 24) and persecution (10:16ff.)? Matthew's community was not about to confuse its present experience with the peace and joy of the parousia. The gospel itself confronts this reality. The full harvest of the kingdom must be awaited. In the meantime, the citizens of the kingdom must be patient with the ambiguities of weeds among the grain (cf. Matt 13:37-43). The dragnet of God's kingdom in the world collects all sorts of things, good and bad. The sorting must await the end (cf. Mt 13:47-50). There will be wars, persecutions, sufferings of all sorts; and worst of all, even within the community "love will grow cold" (cf. 24:1-1 3).

Is, then, Matthew's interpretation of the death of Jesus as the beginning of the new age a false hope? The gospel's conviction is unshaken. The new age *has* dawned. Those who continue Jesus' ministry of the kingdom are continuing a process of conversion which will inevitably lead to victory and the final consummation (24:14) . The commission given to the community is a commission confident of victory: "Full authority has been given to me both in heaven and on earth; go therefore, and make disciples of all the nations" (28:18-19).

But how does the community sustain this conviction? And what is its guarantee that the new age has dawned?

Matthew's firmest answer is the community's experience of the presence of the Risen Lord in its midst. His very name is "Emmanuel," God with us (1:23). Wherever the community gathers, no matter how insignificant its numbers, the Risen Lord is in its midst (18:18). And no matter how long it must endure, it does not lose heart, because it knows that the Risen Lord, God's Son, is with it always, until the end of the world (28:20). The members of the community draw their strength and hope from this presence.

In their midst, too, begin to erupt signs and symptoms of the final reign of God: the sick are healed, the ignorant are taught, offenders are forgiven, enemies are loved.

Thus Matthew's statement about the meaning of Jesus's death as the beginning of the new age is ultimately a statement about the destiny of the Christian community.

Notes

1. Redaction criticism has generated a number of studies on Matthew's passion narrative. See, for example, N. A. Dahl, "Die Passionsgeschichte bei Matthaus," *New Testament Studies* 2 (1955-.56): 17-32; A. Descamps, "Redaction et christologie dans le recit mattheen de la Passion," in M. Didier (ed.), *L'Evangile selon Matthieu, Rédaction et théologie* (Gembloux, 1972), pp. 359-415. A survey of recent studies can be found in D. Senior, "The Passion Narrative in the Gospel of Matthew," in Didier (ed.), *L'Evangile selon Matthieu,* pp. 343-57.

2. Fuller studies of the role of Psalm 22 in the passion tradition can be found in H. Gese, "Psalm 22 und das Neue Testament. Der alteste Bericht vom Tode Jesus und die Entstehung des Herrenmahles," *Zeitschrift fur Theologie und Kirche* 65 (1968): 1-22 (English summary in *Theology Digest* 18 (1970): 237-243); J. H. Reumann, "Psalm 22 at the Cross, Lament and Thanksgiving for Jesus Christ," *Interpretation* 28 (1974): 39-58; D. Senior, "A Death Song," *The Bible Today* (Feb. 1974), pp. 1457-63.

3. For a discussion of this point, see J. R. Donahue, *Are You the Christ?* (SBL Dissertation Series 10) (University of Montana Press, 1973), pp. 201-6.

4. Perhaps the most comprehensive study of this passage in recent literature is the unpublished dissertation of D. Hutton, "The Resurrection of the Holy Ones (Mt 27:51b-53): A Study of the Theology of the Matthean Passion Narrative" (Cambridge, Mass., 1970).

5. Quoted from the edition of R. H. Charles, *The Apocrypha and Pseudepigrapha of the Old Testament* (Oxford, 1913), 218-.19.

6. Cf. J. Grassi, "Ezekiel XXXVII. 1-14 and the New Testament," *New Testament Studies* 11 (1964-65): 162-64.

7. Cf. Y. Yadin's account of the scroll's discovery in *Masada, Herod's Fortress and the Zealots' Last Stand* (London, 1971), pp. 187-89.

8. A detailed study of the panel is found in the article of R.

Wischnitzer-Bernstein, "The Conception of the Resurrection in the Ezekiel Panel of the Dura Synagogue," *Journal of Biblical Literature* 60 (1941): 43–55; cf., further, H. Riesenfeld, *The Resurrection in Ezekiel XXXVII and in the Dura-Europos Paintings* (Uppsala Universitets Arsskrift 11) (Uppsala, 1948).

The Desolation of Jesus in the Gospel

Patrick Rogers C.P.
St. Joseph's Retreat
Mt. Argus, Dublin

The Cry of Dereliction

I‍t is a common feature of the biographer's art to report some final utterance of the great man in question. The writers of the Old Testament offer many examples of this convention. We read the solemn last words of Moses (Dt 33:2-29) and of David the king. The old patriarch Mattathias, the father of the Maccabees, is likewise credited with some unforgettable words of zeal and inspiration just before his death, urging his sons to bring to success the war of freedom he had begun (I Macc 2:49-69). The New Testament, too, offers several examples of this tradition. As one example we may note that Luke, in Acts 7:59-60, is careful to report the final and glorious words of the first Christian martyr, Stephen. Thus it is not surprising that the gospels should round off their story of the mortal life of Jesus by reporting his last words on the cross. However, the traditions behind the words in the gospels are very different, and pose a knotty problem of reconciliation for any exegete who attempts to defind the historicity of all the "seven last words."[1]

Mt 27:46 and Mk 15:34 report the cry of dereliction or abandonment: "My God, my God, why did you forsake me?" Luke presents the last words of Jesus rather differently, as full of forgiveness for the executioners and the good thief, and of devout trust in God as a Father who receives Jesus' final self-offering (Lk 23:34 46). John completes his gospel portrait of the majestic Word and Son of God by showing Jesus serene

55

and regal upon the cross: entrusting Mary to the Beloved Disciple, requesting a drink so as to fulfill yet
another prophecy of the Scriptures, and finally declar-
ing that all was now achieved according to the command of his Father and freely handing over his spirit
(Jn 19:26-30).

Readers of the gospels usually find the cry of dereliction most difficult to integrate into their previous
ideas of Jesus. That cry tends to shock our notion of
the calm, masterful Christ—the Jesus, for example, of
John's gospel—and to show him near desperation. Many
commentators in the past have held that Luke deliberately replaced the cry of Mk 15:34 with the more
edifying prayer, "Into your hands I commend my spirit," a prayer taken straight from the best Old Testament tradition.[2]

Despite the problem it raises, the cry of dereliction
exerts a fascination on the reader. If it repels, it can
also attract. Words that seem to show Jesus abandoned
and totally crushed may well cause us to reformulate
our ideas of the hypostatic union, but they also comfort us with his total identity with suffering man. In
a word, as Charles Journet has written, the cry in Mk
15:34 "reveals to us the ultimate depth of the mystery
of the Incarnation, and of the abasement of the Word-
made-Flesh."[3]

Past Interpretations

The particular "last word" of Jesus which we are
considering has been submitted to careful examination
by many Christians in the centuries since Mark wrote
it into his gospel. Others have written in detail on the
exegetical history of this verse;[4] we simply outline the

mainstreams of opinion, ancient, medieval, and modern.

In the earliest centuries, among the fathers of the Church, some interpreted the cry of Jesus in a purely *metaphorical* sense, with Jesus speaking in the name of sinful humanity but not in his own name. Sinful mankind, mysteriously bound up with the person of Jesus, abandoned by God. Thus Origen, Athanasius, and Cyril of Alexandria. Augustine develops this explanation at some length in his commentary on Psalm 22. The cry of dereliction was indeed spoken by Jesus, but not in his capacity as head, rather in the name of his body, that is, the Church, and sinful humanity in general. "For God did not desert Christ . . . rather, it was man who was abandoned by God, that is to say, it was sinful Adam."[5] The body, in whose name Jesus speaks, is "our old Adam, fastened with Christ to the cross."

Other fathers preferred to interpret the cry more simply and *literally*. These, including Tertullian, Ambrose, and Jerome, accepted the notion that Jesus, in his psychic and human consciousness, truly felt abandoned by the Father. His anguish was real, though it existed by his own consent. He willed to experience the full human tragedy of death, and was indeed abandoned into the hands of sinful man.

In medieval times some scholars accepted and expanded the figurative interpretation of the verse, while others took the literal sense and pushed it to the extremes. Thomas Aquinas, with his usual clarity, distinguished between total and partial abandonment. He thus concludes that Jesus was abandoned by God, not by any break in their divine union but by his human exposure to suffering and death. His abandonment was "not in regard to suffering."[6]

"Abandonment" was taken more literally by other theologians, following the lead of Anselm of Canterbury's *Cur Deus Homo*? Anselm's theology of salvation held that Jesus was abandoned in order to satisfy the angry justice of God. Stress was placed on the suffering servant text of Is 53:6, "The Lord laid upon him the iniquity of us all," and upon the "curse" which Gal 3:13 says Jesus endured for our sake.

Pushing this interpretation yet further, the theologians of the Reformation developed a one-sided view of soteriology through an overemphasis of *satisfaction* or *penal substitution*. Martin Luther, for example, speaks of Jesus on the cross as "at the same time supremely just and supremely sinful, supremely radiant and supremely desperate, supremely happy and supremely accursed (*damnatum*)."[7]

John Calvin insists that Jesus experienced every terror: "horror and dismay which forced him to pray to avoid death." But in order to placate the anger of God, Jesus had to bear the intolerable weight of the divine curse and be subjected to a feeling of damnation.[8] For Calvin, the cry of desolation was but the existential utterance of what seemed to him a basic element in soteriology, that the cross is penalty, separation, almost total (but short-lived) enmity between Jesus and God.

It should be noted that today's Protestant exegetes have, for the most part, dissociated themselves from the extremes of this early Reformation soteriology. Vincent Taylor, to give but one example, is careful to dismiss the notion that Jesus was abandoned by the Father, or that he endured the pains of the lost as a substitute for sinners. He refers to this as "the traditional theory . . . of Luther, more cautiously expressed by Calvin."[9]

Modern Interpretations

Modern interpretations of the cry of desolation can be generally divided according to two main trends, one of which lays stress on the notion of desolation while the other tends to emphasize the idea of prayerful trust.[10] Those who stress the desolate abandonment of the cry are careful to avoid a crude version of the penal substitution theory, but speak of Jesus' anguish at feeling temporarily separated from God by his solidarity with human misery and sin. Other exegetes, taking a different approach in explaining the cry, interpret it in the whole context of Psalm 22. While not excluding the real grief experienced by Jesus, they see him enduring it in an attitude of profound prayer—the kind of endurance that is such a notable feature of the Old Testament psalms of lament.

In order to appreciate the force of this "prayerful" interpretation of Mk 15:34 it is necessary to digress to consider Psalm 22 in its full meaning. It is one of the classic Old Testament lamentation psalms, a genre which has a deep-rooted tradition in Israel's prayer.[11] We find outspoken laments by Moses (Ex 5:22-23), Joshua (Jos 7:7-9), Gideon (Jgs 6:13), Jeremiah (Jer 4:10), and Job (Jb 29-31). In all these texts the speakers pour out their complaint against God, who has left them disappointed. Their frank expression of a sense of grievance against Yahweh was, in context, hardly a sign of desperation but rather an indication of robust faith. Believing, as they did, in the Lord's almighty power, and in his personal care for Israel and in the just, they gave voice to aggrieved perplexity when he apparently allowed their enemies to triumph.

They question God in full expectation of a favorable reply. Consider: "Why do you look on faithless men, and remain silent while the wicked swallow up the righteous?" (Hab 1:13); or "O hope of Israel . . . why are you like a stranger in the land . . . like a mighty warrior who cannot save?" (Jer 14:8-9).

This questioning lamentation recurs very often in the Psalter. The psalmist asks God, "Why do you cast us off forever? Why does your anger smoke hot against the sheep of your pasture?"(Ps 74:1); "Why do you hide your face? Why forget our affliction and opporession?" (Ps 44:24); or again, "How long, O Lord? Will you forget me forever? . . . How long shall my enemy be exalted over me?" (Ps 13:1-2).

Candid openness was part of Israelite piety, and was far from expressing either rebellion against Yahweh's will or despair of his help. The aggrieved question was truly an anguished prayer, but less a challenge than a request for immediate help.

In this prayer-tradition, the first complaint of Psalm 22 begins to take on fuller meaning. It does not indicate despair or even a weakening of the speaker's adherence to God.

We can go further along this line of interpretation by recalling the usual structure of the lamentation psalms.[12] The structure is rather simple, consisting of only three parts: (a) an introduction, in which God's name is invoked in a cry of distress; (b) a main section, in which the psalmist's distress is outlined and his prayer for relief is said; and (c) a conclusion, which expresses the psalmist's trust and thanksgiving, confident that God has heard him.

This threefold structure is well exemplified in the psalm from the cross. After the introduction (Ps 22:1-2), the main section (vv. 3-21) alternates between pathetic expressions of misery and appeals for help from God, who has saved in the past: "In you our fathers trusted . . . upon you was I cast from my birth . . . be not far from me when trouble is near . . . O you, my help, hasten to my aid." The conclusion (vv. 22-31) is a radiant hymn of joy that God has heard, and is intervening to save his faithful servant: "He has not despised or abhorred the affliction of the afflicted; he has not hidden his face from him, but heard when he cried to him . . . Those who seek him shall praise the Lord!"

The whole of Psalm 22 appears to have been seen in the early Christian Church as having prophetic value, pointing forward to Jesus and to his passion. Along with the servant songs of Isaiah, this psalm ranks among the foremost of the "testimonies," those Old Testament passages that were in frequent use by the early Christians to support their faith in Jesus as the long-awaited Messiah.[13] In using these testimonies the Church wished to affirm that the passion was not a bleak tragedy, but the fulfillment of God's preordained design. Paul tells us, following the very basic tradition of the Church, that "Jesus Christ died . . . according to the Scriptures" (I Cor 15:3). One of the most used scriptural sources for authenticating this claim was Psalm 22.[14]

Verses or phrases from this psalm are quoted by various New Testament writers, and notably by the author of Hebrews: "I will declare your name to my brethren; in the midst of the congregation I will praise you" (Heb 2:12). Within the passion narratives of the gospels are few explicit Old Testament quotations, but we find several clear allusions to Psalm 22. For instance, "They mocked him" (Ps 22:7; cf. Lk 23:35); "They wagged their heads" (Ps 22:7; cf. Mk 15:29); "Let him deliver him" (Ps 22:8; cf. Mt 27:43); "They divided my garments" (Ps 22:18; cf. Mk 15:24, Jn 19:24); and the reference to thirst (Ps 22:15-16). We can see, as C. H. Dodd has remarked, that "the psalm as a whole was clearly regarded as a source of testimonies to the Passion of Christ . . . and probably from an early date, since it is woven into the texture of the Passion Narratives."[15]

It is in view of this deliberate use of Psalm 22 to evoke the Old Testament predictions of the passion that some radical critics doubt, or totally reject, the historicity of the cry of derelicton. They doubt that the bystanders at Calvary ever heard Jesus say "My God, my God, why did you forsake me?"

The Historicity of Mark 15:34

It is believed by some modern scholars that this verse is a theological attribution by Mark to the dying Jesus to underline his piety and fidelity to the cross. Such a view has its roots in the work begun in the last century by D.F. Strauss, whose *Life of Jesus* initiated a radically new phase of New Testament studies. Refusing to believe that a personality so great as Jesus could utter a desperate cry at his death, Strauss explained that the cry of desolation was put upon the lips of Jesus by his followers precisely because, by then, Psalm 22 was being read as a prophetic program of the passion. Among the many exegetes who have since adopted this explanation is R. Bultmann, who maintains that, in the very earliest tradition of the crucifixion narrative, only a wordless cry of Jesus was reported; later tradition supplied the various words cited by the four gospels. More explicitly, B. H. Barnscombe writes: "The desire to fill in the content of the cry must have been very strong. With Psalm 22 so much in the minds of those who preserved and transmitted the story . . . the opening words may have supplied the wording recorded."[16]

This line of argument was rejected by other scholars, including M. J. Lagrange, Vincent Taylor, and perhaps a majority of commentators.[17] But Taylor, is surely exaggerating when he holds that the "effect of shock" that is produced in the reader of Mk 15:34 is such that the early Church must have included it rather reluctantly in the passion narrative, and that "tradition would never have ascribed such a saying to Jesus, except under the warrant of the best testimony."[18] To the ears of the early Christian community, attuned to every echo of the Old Testament, there would be no shock in hearing their master pray the words of a psalm of deepest piety at the hour of his death. The prayer would certainly have sounded less scandalous to them than to Strauss, Taylor, or modern Christians generally.

Instead of aligning ourselves for or against the historicity of the cry, we can more fruitfully underline its deliberate ambiguity and see it as a key to the whole style of Mark's passion narrative. Mark tells, in blunt, harsh language, a story which seems, on the face of it, scandalous: the violent and humiliating death of Jesus, the healing preacher and wonder-worker. Yet, to one who can look deeper and penetrate to the reality beneath the scandalous appearance, Mark shows the passion as a glorious event, as God's victory over evil, the triumph of Jesus through patience.

The Passion: Obscurity, Shot through with Light

Mark's passion story is not isolated but is rather the culmination of his gospel, which has been aptly termed a "Passion account with a long introduction."[19] Mark declares his intent from the start; he is to tell the "good news" of Jesus Christ, the Son of God (Mk 1:1). Yet in the first half of his gospel he represents Jesus as veiling his identity as Messiah from the crowds.[20] And in the second half (from 8:30 onward) he deepens the mystery by constant reference to the coming passion of the "Son of Man." From the beginning of the second chapter, Mark shows Jesus in serious conflict with the established religious leaders, and in 2:20 there is dark reference to the days when the bridegroom will be taken away. This pointer to the eventual cross is clarified at the end of this early series of controversies surrounding Jesus, when the "Pharisees went out and held counsel with the Herodians how to destroy him" (Mk 3:6).

Even earlier, in the first chapter, Mark suggests the struggle and contradiction which will characterize the saving work of Jesus: the spiritual darkness with which he must contend in order to spread the light of his good news. Immediately after the baptism in the Jordan, Mark notes that Jesus "was driven out by the Spirit into the wilderness and was tempted by Satan" (1:13). This account of the temptation, though bare of detail, is filled with significance. In his book, *The Temptation and the Passion,* E. Best describes the intimate connection between these two poles in Jesus' ministry, the one at the beginning, the other at its end.[21] The saving work of Jesus consists precisely in overcoming the power of evil. In the desert, by rejecting temptation, Jesus won a resounding victory over Satan. Yet there remained a further long struggle against evil, to be finally won in the painful victory of Calvary. Paradoxically, Jesus wins this fight precisely by enduring the pain and darkness of death. The darkness on Calvary, which Mark reports (15:33), is an outward sign of this intense struggle; the outcome is similarly indicated by the dramatic rending of the veil of the temple (Mk 15:38), the sign of the dawn of a new age.

Mark delays the revelation of this new dawn until he has narrated the death of Jesus, in all its starkness and horror. The Savior's endurance of mockery, humiliation, suffering, and isolation was full of hidden power. But this power was kept veiled, as was Golgatha itself from the sixth to the ninth hour (Mk 15:33). Jesus last words are in accord with this atmosphere: the prayer of confidence, implicit in Psalm 22 as a whole, is overshadowed by the torment expressed in its opening words, "My God, my God, why did you forsake me?" It remains a prayer of trust and thus an affirmation, rather than a denial, of the continuing essential relationship between Jesus and his Father. But it is also, of all the passages in the Old Testament, the sentence that can most poignantly express the depths of human suffering by which the revelation of that relationship was completed.

With the final breath of Jesus, then, the mystery is bathed in a new light. In a profession of faith that corresponds to the symbolic rending of the temple veil, the Roman centurion says, on behalf of all believers, "Indeed this man was the Son of God" (Mk 15:39). After the deliberate cloak of secrecy in which

Mark has hidden the splendor of Jesus from the temptation to the passion, we have now come full circle to the explicit delcaration of faith with which the evangelist began his gospel: "Jesus Christ, the Son of God" (Mk 1:1). In enduring the passion to the very end, Jesus revealed his divinity in the most surprising but most effective way possible: in the suffering and death of his humanity. He also fulfilled, totally, that mission which he had declared to be his: "The Son of Man has come, not to be served, but to serve, and to give his life as a ransom for many" (Mk 10:45).

The Human Isolation of the Cross

What of the attitude of those whom Jesus came to serve, and for whom he gave his life? In the thought of Mark, Jesus' disciples, too, play a role in the isolation of his death and in the theology of his passion. It is one of the great ironies of Mark that while he insists on the vocation of the disciples to share in the sufferings of Jesus, he shows their master so alone on Golgatha. The only sympathetic onlookers at the crucifixion are the women mentioned in Mk 15:40-41. And even they are described as "looking on *from afar,*" as though Mark were deliberately avoiding the idea that by their presence they were bringing comfort to Jesus.

If we contrast this with the Johannine account of the crucifixion, in which "by the cross of Jesus there stood his mother" with the other women and the Beloved Disciple (Jn 19:25) and take John's version as more probably historical, then Mark is using a dramatist's license to underline the abandonment suffered by Jesus. Not only is he delivered by God "into the hands of men" (Mk 9:31), crucified between two robbers (15:27), with no mention of repentance or sympathy from either, and mocked by the passersby and the chief priests (15:29), but he is totally abandoned by those very disciples who had loudly protested only the night before that they would die rather than desert him (14:31). Instead of carrying out this headstrong pledge, they fulfilled the word of Scripture quoted by Jesus on his way to Gethsemane: "I will strike the shepherd, and the sheep will be scattered" (14:27). Their involvement in his passion would come later, after Pentecost.

The Invitation to Share in His Sufferings

It was axiomatic in the theology of Paul that fruitful apostolic work entailed some share in the sufferings of the Lord.[22] Paul often draws attention to the extraordinary variety of ways in which he himself was tested.[23] Mark, writing about the time of Paul's death, is careful to show that not only the apostles but every one of Jesus' disciples must bear a portion of his sufferings. He derives this teaching from the words of Jesus. Several times he reports almost somber warnings to this effect, principally within chapters 8-10, where Jesus' predictions of his coming passion are most explicit.

Mk 8:34-35 announces the hard terms of discipleship immediately after Jesus' first clear prediction of his approaching sufferings: "If any man will come after me, let him deny himself, take up his cross, and follow me." We may note that Mark, unlike Lk 9:23 (a parallel passage), does not spiritualize the saying about the cross by adding the word "daily"; Mark is more direct and his reference to suffering more literal. The kernel of the passion theology, as it applies to disciples, follows in the next verse: "Whoever would save his life will lose it; and whoever loses his life for my sake and the gospel's, will save it." This verse, quoted almost verbatim by both Matthew and Luke, is closely paralleled in Jn 12:25. It is part of the very earliest gospel tradition. J. Jeremias points to it confidently as an example of the style of speech used by Jesus and notes that it is also a solid indication of the historicity of the passion predictions themselves, for "it is very improbable that Jesus would have prepared his disciples for suffering, if he had not expected that he, too, would suffer."[24]

These words of Jesus are an invitation rather than a threat; they open with the condition "If any man will . . . " It is a choice that Jesus puts before his friends, setting them free again to choose or to reject him. "Nobody can be forced, nobody can even be expected to come. He says rather, *'If* any man' is prepared to spurn all those other offers which come his way in order to follow him . . . When the disciples are halfway along the road of discipleship, they come to another crossroads. Once more they are left free to choose for themselves, nothing is expected of them, nothing forced upon them."[25]

In Mk 9:35 a prediction by Jesus of his suffering is again followed by an allusion to the cross in the life of his disciples, although the reference is not as explicit. The disciples were arguing about precedence and status, "which of them should be the greatest," and received from Jesus a pointed lesson in fraternal humility. The lesson, which is once more in the style of paradox favored by Jesus and faithfully reproduced by Mark, has definite overtones of the passion: "If anyone wishes to be first, he must be the last of all and

the *servant* of all." Later, in one of the most precious
short sayings preserved by Mark, Jesus applies this
servant imagery to himself and to his death: "The Son
of Man has not come to be served, but to serve, and
to give his life as a ransom for many" (10:45). The
call of the disciples to "serve," therefore, is not
limited to hearty and vigorous activism but implies,
with its overtones of Is 53, a readiness to lay down
their lives with Jesus, the suffering servant.

The same challenge, the same opportunity, is presented again in Mk 10:39. The disciples James and
John, ignoring or oblivious of the third passion prediction that Jesus had made a few verses earlier, make
an ambitious request of Jesus. They want for themselves the privileged places in his coming glorious kingdom. Clearly, there was still a notion in their minds
that the kingdom of the Messiah was both imminent
and easy to enter! But instead of a place in the coming kingdom, they are challenged to a share in the
coming passion. As he had done before when linking
discipleship with the acceptance of the cross, Jesus sets
before his followers a clear choice: "Are you able to
drink the cup that I drink, or be baptized with the
baptism that I receive?" When they confidently answer "yes," he guarantees them their share both in
his "cup" and in his "baptism." This is their destiny
as followers of the servant-Messiah. No other form of
discipleship is possible, according to this radical Marcan theology. To quote Bonhoeffer again, "suffering
is the badge of true discipleship . . . it is a joy and
a token of his grace."[26]

Failure and Repentance

That the disciples of Jesus failed to accept his challenge of true discipleship is stressed by Mark in his passion narrative. He is quite frank in describing Peter's betrayal of his master (14:66-72). Indeed, when his account is compared with the parallel narratives of Luke and John, the denials seem even more culpable, in that Mark has them immediately following the condemnation of Jesus by the Sanhedrin and the outrages—the spitting, blows, and mockeries—that were then heaped upon him (14:60-65). Coming at this point, Peter's apostasy sharply emphasizes the isolattion of Jesus in his sufferings.

That Peter, and the other disciples who fled from arrest, were reinstated in their discipleship after the resurrection and that they afterward accepted a real sharing in the cross is an important theme in the New Testament. The return of the disciples to fidelity is presupposed in their post-resurrection mission from Jesus to preach the good news of peace and forgiveness (Mk 16:14-20, Mt 28:16-20, Lk 24:44-49, Jn 20:21-23). And as particular attention was given to Peter's desertion, so is special emphasis placed on his repentance.

Mk 14:72 and Mt 26:74 trace Peter's sorrow to the simple hearing of the cock crow, a reminder of the warning that he would indeed prove traitor (Mk 14:30). Lk 22:61 depicts this moment of conversion as resulting from a brief but significant encounter: "The Lord turned and looked at Peter." Jn 21:15-19 expands the theme still further. After a triple profession of love to balance his triple denial, Peter learns of the trials that are in store for him in his renewed discipleship. Lest the point be missed, John makes a close connection between "by what death he would glorify God" and Jesus' repeated call to discipleship, "Follow me."

Whatever the first motivation of Peter's conversion may have been, he, and presumably the other followers of Jesus, learned well the lesson of discipleship and the carrying of the cross. The experience would later spur Peter to declare in his first epistle: "Christ suffered for you, leaving you an example, that you should follow in his steps" (I Pet 2:21); and to call upon the Christian faithful to show solidarity with those who are undergoing their share in the passion of Jesus, "knowing that the same experience of suffering is required of your brotherhood throughout the world" (I Pet 5:9).

The human isolation of Jesus on Calvary is thus not merely the recording of a tragic fact. The gospels' coupling of discipleship with sharing in the passion of the Lord makes of his lonely corss a continuing challenge to those who claim to follow him. Mark's message to the Church has perennial valve: It is not enough to be "looking on from afar"; sharing in Jesus' sufferings is of the very essence of being a Christian.

Notes

1. The number seven is reached by reckoning three "last words" from Luke and from John (Lk 23:34, 43, 46, Jn 19:26, 28, 30) and one word shared by Matthew and Mark (Mt 27:46, Mk 15:34). Attempted harmonizations of the seven last words into one continuous narrative labor under some historical improbability, and the most immediate difficulties are two. Before being offered the drink of sour wine, did Jesus say "I thirst" or "My

God, my God . . ."? And, at the moment of his death, did
he shout aloud, *without* words, as Matthew and Mark imply, or
"It is finished" (Jn 19:30) or, again, "Father, into your hands
I commend my spirit"? (Lk 23:46). A more serious objection
to such harmonizations is that they ignore the special tone or
atmosphere which characterizes the several Gospel accounts of
our Lord's death.

2. Among the more recent commentators, this deliberate re-
placement by Luke has been maintained by J. Schniewind, *Das
Evangelium nach Markus* (2d ed.; Gottingen, 1952), p. 201; V.
Taylor, *The Gospel According to Mark* (2d ed.; London, 1966),
p. 594; and W. E. Bundy, *Jesus and the First Three Gospels* (Cambridge, Mass., 1955), p. 543.

3. C. Journet, *Les Sept Paroles du Christ en Croix* (Paris, 1950),
p. 83.

4. Cf. L. Sabourin, *Rédemption Sacrificielle* (Bruges, 1961), pp.
80-108. A briefer but very useful history of the interpretation is
offered by P. Benoit in *Passion et Resurrection du Seigneur* (Paris,
1966), pp. 221-23.

5. *Ennarationes in Psalmis, Patrologia Latina,* ed. Migne, 36:693.

6. *Lectura super Evangelium S. Matthei,* ed. Marietti (Rome, 1951),
pp. 365-.66.

7. *Operation in Psalmo 22,* ed. de Wette (1583), 3:330-32.

8. *Institutions de la Religion Chrétienne,* cited in Sabourin, *Rédemption
Sacrificielle,* p. 88.

9. V. Taylor, *Jesus and His Sacrifice* (London, 1937), p. 159.

10. This two-fold classification of modern views on our text is
illustrated by such authors as E. Lohmeyer, B. Weiss, and W.
Hazenzahl, who stress the desolation of Jesus, and by M. J.
Lagrange, P. Benoit, and L. Sabourin, who emphasize the prayerful trust expressed in the verse.

11. H. Gunkel, *Einleitung in die Psalmen* (Gottingen, 1933), has a
long section, "The Psalms of Individual Lamentation," to which
Psalm 22 belongs. These psalms, he says, formed the backbone
of the Psalter, and were so beloved by the people that they penetrated as a vital element into the temple worship.

12. This structure is outlined in more detail by L. Sabourin in
The Psalms: Their Origin and Meaning (New York, 1969), 2:1-5.

13. Among the best writings on the topic of these testimonies are B. Lindars, *New Testament Apologetics: The Doctrinal Significance of the Old Testament Quotations* (London, 1961), and C. H. Dodd, *According to the Scriptures: The Substructure of New Testament Theology* (London, 1952).

14. Dodd, in *According to the Scriptures,* comments on the fifteen most important sources of testimonies in the Old Testament. Foremost and rivaled in importance only by the Isaian "servant of Yahweh" passages, is Psalm 22.

15. Ibid., pp. 97-98.

16. *The Gospel of Mark* (London, 1937), p. 289.

17. *Jesus and His Sacrifice,* p. 161; M. J. Lagrange, *Evangile selon Saint Marc* (Paris, 1929), p. 223. T. Boman cites many other authors who firmly reject any doubting of the historicity of this verse, adding, however, that "while the majority of scholars accept the cry of lament as historical, their interpretations of it are quite diverse"; cf., "Das Letzte Wort Jesu," *Studia Theologica* 17 (1963): 103-8.

18. *The Gospel According to Mark,* p. 594.

19. The phrase was coined, I believe, by M. Kahler, and is quoted by A. Vanhoye in *De Narrationibus Passionis Christi in Evangeliis Synopticis* (Rome, 1970), p. 17.

20. The Markan emphasis on the "messianic secret" has often been noted, and the historicity of this gospel theme has been much attacked and defended since W. Wrede's radical thesis on the subject in 1901. For our purpose here, the important thing is that Mark stresses the mystery in Jesus' identity (cf. Mk 1:34, 44, 3:12, 5:43, 7:36, 8:26). From this paradoxical revelation/concealment duality during the public ministry, we are led to the equally paradoxical chiaroscuro at the crucifixion scene.

21. E. Best, *The Temptation and the Passion: The Marken Soteriology* (London, 1965). Best's conclusion is that, in Mark's portrait of the redemption, Christ's struggle is against *sin,* and not simply (as many authors have held) against *Satan.* He places the victory over Satan in the temptation in the wilderness. The cross is the place where Jesus accepts judgment on behalf of sinful men. It is a struggle, insofar as this judgment involves the willing bearing of bitter suffering and the drinking of the chalice of justice. This soteriology is echoed in the cry of dereliction (cf. p. 158).

22. Cf. E. Schweitzer, "Dying and Rising with Christ," *New Testament Studies* 14 (1967): 1–14.

23. Cf. especially 2 Cor 4:8–11 and 11:23–29. Paul gives the theological significance of these hardships in Gal 2:20: "With Christ I am nailed to the cross; it is no longer I that live, but Christ lives in me" (also cf. 2 Cor 1:5 and Rom 6:4).

24. *New Testament Theology* (New York, 1971), p. 283.

25. D. Bonhoeffer, *The Cost of Discipleship* (London, 1959), p. 77.

26. Ibid., p. 80.

The Laos at the Cross:
Luke's Crucifixion Scene

Jerome Crowe C.P.
Holy Cross Retreat
Templestowe, Victoria
Australia

Even a superficial reading of St. Luke's passion story is enough to remind us how much the Church owes to his distinctive presentation of the last hours of Jesus. Christian devotion has followed its own Spirit-guided instinct in assimilating Luke's particular emphasis on the goodness of Jesus, his kindness to sinners, and his filial prayer—aspects that are strikingly illustrated in the details of the offer of paradise to a repentant sinner and his commendation of his life into the hands of his Father. At the same time, Luke's pictorial approach, his gift for conveying theology through tableaux, has stimulated the efforts of Christian artists and iconographers, and has invited them to take his scenes as their point of departure.

The following pages will concentrate on some other important and distinctive elements of Luke's picture of the death of Christ in an attempt to bring his crucifixion scene into specifically Lucan focus. Luke's tableau differs from those of Matthew and Mark not only in its special material and the particular order in which he arranges items common to all three; it differs particularly in the composition of the scene, especially in the position Luke assigns to the *laos,* the people of God. In the attitudes of the *laos* during and after the crucifixion, we may discover one of the most characteristic features of his picture, namely the framework in which he has enclosed it. The framework suggests the title "The *Laos* at the Cross." Luke places the crucified Christ firmly within the people of God, who are confronted with the abasement of Jesus the Messiah-king, whose death is the final earthly manifestation of his divine sonship.

The Framework

Like all of the evangelists, Luke passes over the act of crucifixion in a word. "When they came to the place which is called the Skull, there they crucified him and the criminals, one on the right and one on the left" (Lk 23:33). Like Matthew and Mark, Luke draws on Psalm 22 in the phrase "And they cast lots to divide his garments" (23:34). But whereas Matthew and Mark find the details of the psalm a useful model in their account of the crucifixion, Luke departs at this point from its text and adapts it radically to obtain a striking contrast. The psalmist had complained, "I am a worm and no man, disgrace of men and object of the contempt of the *laos*. All who behind me mock at me" (Ps 22:7-8; cf. Ps 35:16). Luke makes a significant change and writes, "And the *laos* stood watching, but the rulers mocked him saying, 'He saved others, let him save himself, if he is the Christ of God, his Chosen One'" (23:35). Whereas in Matthew and Mark "those who passed by derided him." Luke differentiates among the audience. For Luke, the rulers mock; the *laos* stands by watching.[1]

"The *laos*" is clearly distinguished from the "rulers." Its attitude distinguishes it similarly from other groups, such as "the high priests and scribes" who, in the earlier episode of the trial before Herod, "stood by, vehemently accusing him" (Lk 23:10), and from all the active participants in the scene. Rulers, soldiers, and the first criminal speak out in mockery and blasphemy, the second criminal in repentance and faith. Even earth and temple are associated in gestures of mourning. Jesus speaks in pardon and prayer. The pagan centurion glorifies God and proclaims the innocence of Jesus.

Luke also departs from his Marcan model after the crucifixion to divide the *laos* into two groups of watchers. Mark and Matthew note the presence of "women looking on from afar" in a description reminiscent of Ps 38:12.[2] Luke enlarges this group by including "acquaintances" of Jesus, evoking reminiscences of other psalms and finding a term to suggest the presence of the disciples, and by drawing attention to "all the crowds who assembled at the spectacle, who, having seen the things that happened, returned beating their breasts" (Lk 23:48).[3]

The crucifixion is thus enclosed within Lk 23:35-49 by an inclusion which has the *laos* standing by and watching at the beginning and two other watching groups at the end. This framework surrounds the death of Jesus on the cross, and is included in the larger frame of Lk 23:26-56, a unit which commences with the way of the cross and concludes with the burial. Persons and events within the inner frame are closely connected with those in the outer frame. The two criminals are introduced in the outer frame, as is the *laos*. "And there followed him a great multitude of the *laos,* and of women who bewailed and lamented him" (Lk 23:27).[4] The crowds who return beating their breasts assume, after the death of Jesus, the attitude of mourning adopted before his death by the women of Jerusalem. Using a favorite refrain, Luke has them "return" to Jerusalem, bringing them back to the city which is the center of action and the point where they began.

The crucifixion is similarly connected with the episode of the burial which follows. "And all his acquaintances and the women who had followed him from Galilee stood at a distance and saw these things" (Lk 23:49).[5] The acquaintances of Jesus, and the women, have yet other things to see. It is not until the women have "seen the tomb and how the body was placed" that they also "return" in order to prepare for their last ministry to Jesus.

The whole section is part of the larger passion story of Luke, so that we can move outward from the details of the inner frame to place the crucifixion within the setting of Luke's two-volume work, studying it not only in its details but in the place which Luke assigns to it within the vast panorama which includes, on one canvas, the road from Jerusalem to Rome and a time span of three decades. In this way we may hope to shed some light on the place of the cross in the work of salvation as Luke conceives it and ask what his manner of presentation may have meant to the people for whom it was destined.

Luke's Use of the Term Laos

The word *laos* is a favorite term of Luke's. Of its 140 occurrences in the New Testament, 84 are to be found in Luke-Acts, 36 of them in the gospel. Outside Luke, its commonest meaning is the generic one of "people, populace, crowd." Luke's usage is distinctive and is influenced by the Septuagint, whose translators chose a term that was used in this generic way in profane literature and carefully restricted it to Israel.

They thus endowed the word *laos* with a new status and significance. It became the specific term which emphasized the special and privileged position of Israel as Yahweh's convenant people, "the people of Yahweh."

When he uses the term in the plural, Luke is employing it in its profane sense of "people" or "nations," but otherwise the term *laos* in the gospel of Luke generally retains its religious connotation of "people of God."[6] Since this is so, he needs another word for "crowd" and uses the term *ochlos,* which is especially frequent in the central section of his gospel, where the term *laos* simply disappears. Yet the *laos* is not synonymous with the *ochlos,* any more than either is synonymous with the other prominent group, the "disciples."

The Infancy Gospel

The reader first meets the *laos* in the impressive opening tableau which Luke places in Jerusalem, in the temple, at the hour of the afternoon offering of incense. "All the multitude of the *laos*" are found onstage in a posture of prayer and expectation (Lk 1:10, 21). Inside the temple, Zechariah hears from the angel that the mission of his son will be "to make ready for the Lord a *laos* prepared" (Lk 1:17). In his exit lines, he praises God who has "visited and redeemed his *laos*" (Lk 1:68). In the angelic visitation to the shepherds, the birth of Jesus is proclaimed as "good news of great joy which will come to all the *laos*" (Lk 2:10).[7]

The people of God are introduced as a group, but also in a number of representative figures who embody the group's ideal features.[8] They include Zechariah and Elizabeth (Lk 1:16), the prophetess Anna (2:36), Simeon (2:25), Mary and Joseph (2:28). These men and women are models of piety, prayer, worship, and hopeful expectation, the things that constitute Israel as the people of God, and they are clustered like satellites around the central figure of Mary, herself the personification of the *laos* in her humble acceptance of God's word in faith. The angel addresses her in terms the prophets had used in proclaiming their message of hope to the "daughter of Zion."[9]

The mission of Jesus is defined mainly in terms of the salvation of God's people (cf. Lk 1:32, 69).[10] Yet Simeon announces that "my eyes have seen your salvation which you have prepared in the presence of all peoples, a light for revelation to the gentiles, and for glory to your people Israel" (Lk 2:30-32). He has hardly proclaimed the child as Israel's glory before he points out the paradoxical way in which his mission will be accomplished. He prophesies to Mary: "This child is set for the fall and rise of many in Israel and for a sign that is spoken against (and a sword will pierce through your own soul also) that thoughts out of many hearts may be revealed" (Lk 2:34f). The sword of God's judgment will pass through the heart of Israel; the ministry of Jesus will lay bare the deepest attitudes of men to God.[11]

As he begins Luke's two-volume work, the reader is shown the mystery of Jesus in all the light that the resurrection has thrown on it and that a half-century of Christian reflection had come to appreciate. In his own faith in resurrection, the reader holds the key to the understanding of these events; the participants do not. Their responses show them involved in a mystery too profound for their grasp. The *laos* reacts to the initial events with wonder, amazement, fear (Lk 1:21, 65; 2:18, 47). At the finding of Jesus in the temple, Luke says of even Joseph and Mary: "when they saw him, they were astonished" (2:48).[12] "They did not understand (2:50) the first recorded words of Jesus, his revelation in act of his divine sonship and of the overriding claims of the mission of his heavenly Father which call him to the temple. In the presence of this mystery, "his mother kept all these things in her heart" (2:51).

The Ministry of John

Luke describes the ministry of John in terms that show it as the fulfillment of Gabriel's words to Zechariah. By his apocalyptic preaching of impending judgment and of Israel's need to make ready for it, John brings into being a *laos* prepared for the coming of Jesus. His harshest words are aimed at complacency in Israel's privileged position as "children of Abraham," the facile assumption that they are natural or automatic heirs to the covenant promises by right of birth.

The *laos* John prepares is not coterminous with the nation of Israel. While it includes the "crowds," the "tax collectors," and "soldiers," to whom he spells out the demands of penance (Lk 3:7, 10, 12, 14), Luke makes a clear distinction between those who "justified God" by accepting John's baptism and those, like the Pharisees and the lawyers, who "rejected the purpose of God for themselves, not having been baptized by him" (7:29), and the "high priests, scribes, and priests'' who refused to acknowledge that John's baptism was of God (30:1).[13]

John's ministry thus sets in motion the eschatological process of Israel's division. He brings out the expectations of the *laos* and rejects its unspoken identification of himself as the Messiah. Our last glimpse of John shows him "with many other exhortations, preaching good news to the *laos*" (Lk 3:18). Thus Luke sets the scene for the entrance of Jesus, who takes his place among the *laos* John has prepared and accepts his solidarity with them by accepting the rite of baptism. In Luke 3:21 Jesus is invested as messianic king and as Son of God; he commences his mission to an Israel already divided into a people prepared for his coming and those who have not responded to the message of John.

These scenes of the ministry of John and the baptism of Jesus are set in the midst of the *laos* in an entirely Jewish background. But several hints point to the universality of the "purpose of God" that is being implemented. Luke describes John in a quotation from Isaiah which was traditional and is employed by the other three evangelists, but he carries the quotation beyond the point at which Mark leaves it, so as to include the prophetic words "and all flesh shall see the salvation of God" (Lk 3:6). His insistence on God's ability to "raise up children to Abraham from these stones" (3:8) points to the *laos* that will come into existence by God's initiative, irrespective of birth into the Jewish people. The story of the baptism of Jesus that underlines his solidarity with the Jewish *laos* is followed immediately by Luke's genealogy that underlines his solidarity with the whole human race (3:23-37).

The Ministry of Jesus

The reaction of the people of Nazareth, which Luke places almost at the beginning of Jesus' ministry, is a clear example of the process of division and discernment of hearts which Simeon had prophesied (Lk 4:16-30). From the Book of Isaiah Jesus reads the promise of good news to the poor, remission of sentence to prisoners, sight to the blind. This promise he proclaims as fulfilled "today," as a reality present in his ministry, to which his townsmen are summoned to respond. They "wonder at the words of grace" he speaks but are incapable of recognizing him as anything but the son of Joseph. When he talks of God's past favors to the gentiles, they are enraged to the point of murder.

His coming lays bare the attitudes of men. His claim to forgive sins provokes scribes and Pharisees to the judgment that he is a blasphemer (Lk 5:21); they judge him a breaker of the Law because his disciples pluck grain on the Sabbath (6:2); they watch him to see whether he will heal on the Sabbath, to find an accusation against him. Jesus knows their thoughts, and they were "filled with fury and discussed with one another what they might do to Jesus" (6:7, 11).

The *laos* appears several times in this section, the "crowd" or "crowds" more often. It is difficult to maintain the distinction between them, though both are clearly differentiated from the group of disciples. (The latter are set apart by a personal call of Jesus, inviting them to a closer permanent relationship with him.) In no instance other than that of Nazareth does Jesus encounter hostility from either *laos* or crowd. Their response is uniformly favorable. The crowds "sought him out and came to him and would have kept him from leaving them" (Lk 4:42). "Great crowds" come to him to hear him and to be cured, to touch him, press upon him, follow after him, and welcome him (6:19; 7:9, 11, 12; 8:40). His miracles cause them to "glorify God" and to exclaim that "a great prophet has risen among us," "God has visited his people," "We have seen strange things today" (5:16; 7:16). But the events are too great for them; they are "troubled," "beside themselves," in fear and wonder (4:32; 5:26; 9:43).

That the disciples have penetrated further into the mystery of Jesus than the crowds is shown by the disciples' response to the double question, "Who do the crowds say that I am?" and "But who do you say that I am?" (Lk 9:19, 20). But, even so, when Jesus announces his death for the first time "they did not understand this saying and it was concealed from them, that they should not perceive it, and they were afraid to ask him about this saying" (9:45).

When Jesus "sets his face steadfastly toward Jerusalem" on the journey to his death, he turns to address the disciples and the crowd who follow (Lk 9:55; 10:24; 14:25).[15] The *laos* is absent from these chapters, but the theme of division is no less clear and is sounded in such statements as "as he said this, all his adversaries were put to shame; and all the crowd rejoiced at the glorious things that were done by him" (13:17).[16] His adversaries include the scribes and Pharisees, who "press him hard to provoke him to speak of many things, lying in wait for him, to catch at something he might say," and who murmur at his welcome to sinners (11:53; 15:2). Jesus reduces the Pharisees to silence, and brands Pharisees and lawyers alike as "hypocrites" in a series of woes (11:39-44, 45-52). At the same time, his maledictions extend beyond these restricted groups to take in entire towns that remain impenitent despite the signs offered to them, and above all Jerusalem, the unfaithful city of God whose conversion he has so longed for and which will consummate its centuries of infidelity by putting him to death (10:13-15; 13:33-35).

The process of division is seen even in the crowds who gather in their thousands, "follow" him, or "journey with him" (Lk 7:9; 9:11; 12:1; 14:25). Some begin to ascribe his cures to an alliance with Beelzebul and others test him by seeking a sign from heaven (11:14, 16, 17). Jesus refutes their charge and refuses to offer to "this evil generation" any other sign than himself. In tones comparable to those of the Baptist he calls the crowds, too, "hypocrites" for their ignorance of the impending judgment (12:54-59).

Luke has consistently distinguished the disciples from the crowd, and he continues to do so. Much of the matter of this section of his gospel is instruction about discipleship. The section is headed by three episodes explaining the demands which Jesus makes on his disciples (Lk 9:57-62). We hear of the mission of the seventy, and the jubilant prayer of Jesus on their return (10:1-10, 17-21). The disciples are the subjects of a special beatitude; they have "seen and heard what many prophets and kings desired to see and hear" (11:23-24). For them Jesus reserves both his teaching on prayer (11:1-13; 18:1-8) and the eschatological discourse of 17:22-.37. Still, when he tells them again of his coming sufferings, "they understood none of these things, this saying was hid from them, and they did not grasp what was said" (18:33).

The situation at the end of the journey can be summarized thus: the mission of Jesus is a sign offered to an evil generation. His adversaries have rejected it. The crowds, generally favorable, are nonetheless divided. The disciples follow him to Jerusalem, believing in him as Messiah's suffering. The events in Jerusalem will clarify the lines along which Israel is divided. Luke will simplify the division as one between *laos* and leaders.

The Events in Jerusalem

The *laos* returns repeatedly to the stage in the last five chapters of the gospel.[17] Near Jericho, toward the end of his journey, Jesus cures a blind man, an act which presages his opening of the blind eyes of the disciples. The blind man, healed, follows Jesus, glorifying God, "and all the *laos*, when they saw it, gave praise to God" [Lk 18:43]. At the end of the journey, Jesus enters Jerusalem as Israel's King and takes possession of the temple. Luke is at pains to forestall any misunderstanding about the nature of that kingship, and has Jesus tell the parable about the nobleman who went on a long journey to obtain kingship for himself "and to return" (19:11-27). Jesus' triumphant entry, which follows, is not to be seen as the return of the victorious king to his city but as part of Jesus' long journey through death and resurrection to his exaltation as messianic king.

In Luke's story, Jesus is explicity saluted as king by "the whole multitude of the disciples" (19:37). The song of the angels at Jesus' birth has spread to his disciples. It is in the midst of this rejoicing that Jesus, in tears, proclaims the judgment of Israel's king on his city, which is ranked among "those enemies of mine, which did not want me to reign over them" (19:27), and doomed to destruction because it has not recognized "the time of its visitation" (19:44).[18]

In the temple, the Messiah gathers the *laos* about him, "teaching and proclaiming the good news." The *laos* "listens to him gladly" and "comes to him in the temple in the morning to hear him" (Lk 19:48; 21:37). This coming reverses earlier roles: now the leaders and teachers of Israel approach Jesus to ask him questions; they wonder at his answers, and are silent (20:26, 40). To the question of "chief priests, scribes, and elders" about his authority, Jesus responds with a counter-question about John's baptism, in which he had been invested with the authority of messianic king and Son of God, which he is at the moment exercising (20:1-8). To the *laos* he addresses the parable of the wicked vineyard keepers whose murderous intentions are finally revealed at the coming of the "beloved Son," thus assuring their own destruction and the letting of God's vineyard to others (20:9-18). In the hearing of the *laos* he utters his condemnation of the scribes (30:45).

Before the passion begins, the *laos* has been carefully distinguished from those who are responsible for the death of Jesus. The scribes and the chief priests recognize the parable as aimed at them and they seek to kill Jesus, but are deterred by their fear of the *laos* (Lk 21:19; 22:2). They cannot trap him in his speech in the presence of the *laos* (20:26). In a series of nine episodes, *laos* and leaders are distinguished.[19] The leaders seek his death; the *laos* is a group friendly to Jesus, which "listens" to his word that goes out from the temple (20:45).

The Crucifixion Scene

The crucifixion scene in Luke's passion story is the peak point in the continuing process of division. The "spectacle" of the crucified Christ brings out the inner dispositions of the participants. His last hours seem a violent contradiction of all the solemn titles bestowed on him in the infancy narrative. Luke has presented the Jewish trial in a way that brings out the divine sonship of Jesus, who is condemned on his own testimony that he is the Son of God. This leaves Luke free to present the crucifixion in a way that emphasizes the kingship of Jesus.[20] The insults to which Jesus is subjected are directed principally at his claim to be the Messiah. He is mocked by the rulers for his claim to be the Christ of God, the Chosen One. The soldiers mock at his claim to be the king of the Jews, and the title above his head adds its own mute mockery. The first of the two criminals mocks him for his claim to be the Christ. All, without exception, mock him in his title of Savior. As the *laos* stands by, it is confronted by the terrible contradiction between his crucified state and its own expectations of him. It contemplates in the crucified Christ a Savior who cannot save himself, let alone others.

The process of division finally touches the persons closest to Jesus. In the passion stories of Matthew and Mark, the two thieves crucified with Jesus revile him (Mt 27:44); Mk 15:32).[21] Luke has a final distinction to make. When the abasement of Jesus has reached its nadir in the blasphemy of the first thief, the second makes a last-hour profession of faith in the kingship of Jesus, whose innocence he proclaims as he invokes the clemency of the crucified Christ, whom he, alone of all present, openly acknowledges as king. The last royal gesture of Jesus is an offer of release to this captive, whom he promises to associate with himself in paradise "today." The elements join in the mourning com-

menced by the women of Jerusalem, an eclipse of the
sun clothes the earth in darkness, and the temple, rends
its garments. His gesture to the criminal has been a
last revelation of Jesus crucified as king; his last prayer
is his final revelation of himself as Son. With his ha-
bitual trust, he prays to the God, whom he persists to
the end in calling "Abba" (Father), and commends his
life into the hands of a Father who has shown him
how far the demands of sonship can lead.

"And the *laos* stood by, watching." Like Mary in
the temple, it does not understand. It stands by, watching the spectacle, until Jesus' earthly life is over. The
crowds are moved to something that Luke, careful artist
that he is, still does not call repentance, though it is
to become so after Pentecost.[22] Of the group that stands
"at a distance," the women see Jesus laid in the tomb.
All the "seeing" that is possible in his earthly life is
completed.

The Resurrection and Beyond

The final chapter of the gospel shows how the Risen
Christ finally opens the eyes of the disciples to penetrate the mystery. The eyes of the travelers on the
road to Emmaus are still "held so as not to recognize Jesus"; they are disillustioned in their hope "that
he was the one to redeem Israel" because of his
death—still incapable, as they are, of believing "all
that the prophets have spoken" (Lk 24:16, 21, 25).
Jesus explains the Scriptures to them, and in the breaking of the bread "their eyes were opened and they
recognized him" (24:26, 31). In his later appearance
to the disciples, he opens their eyes to recognize his
presence. When they are "afraid that they are seeing

a spirit," he offers them his hands to see, invites them to "touch and see," to recognize in him the crucified Jesus (24:37, 39).

At the same time, he "opens their minds" to understand at last the mystery of the suffering Messiah as it is revealed in the Scriptures (Lk 24:45). Then he can commission them as his "witnesses" to proclaim "penance and forgiveness of sins in his name to all nations, beginning from Jerusalem" (24:47).

Luke's second volume shows the commission carried into effect. The Acts of the Apostles describes the ultimate stage in the process of division within Israel that led to the constitution of the *laos* which Luke knew. He sketches the stages of that development, beginning with the preaching of the "witnesses" at Pentecost as members of a group which regarded itself as part of the *laos* it addressed. Like Jesus, they enjoy the favor of the *laos* (Acts 2:47). The apostles continue the teaching and preaching of Jesus to the *laos* (Acts 4:2, 5; 12:20); the miracles they work "in the name of Jesus" fill the *laos* with wonder and anazement (Acts 3:10); and their ministry divides *laos* from leaders as surely as did that of Jesus (Acts 4:14; 4:17, 21; 5:13-17, 26).

To the people of Jerusalem they preach the crucifixion as a motive for repentance. They recall the circumstances of the death of Jesus to bring home to them their sin and their responsibility for his death. This theme recurs four times in the early chapters, and Luke shows the efficacy of this preaching of the cross in mass conversions (Acts 2:22f. 36; 3:13f., 17, 19; 4:10-12).[23] It is true that only the resurrection and the word of the witnesses could unveil the dignity of Jesus; so Israel's sin can be ascribed to ignorance (Acts 3:17; 13:27). But the time of ignorance is past with the preaching of the witnesses. In the resurrection God has raised up the prophet of whom Moses spoke; the threat of Deuteronomy has become a reality: "It shall be that every soul that does not listen to that prophet shall be destroyed from the *laos*" (cf. Acts 3:23).

By the time that Luke wrote, the separation of the Christian community from the mother body of Israel was long since complete. The declaration of James at the Council of Jerusalem was an official recognition of the manifest fact of the mission to the pagans: "God has visited the Gentiles to take out of them a *laos* for his name" (Acts 15:14).[24] Right to the concluding tableau of his second volume, Luke insists on the division brought about in Israel as the preachers of the gospel confront it with the mystery of Jesus. This final tableau is a picture of Paul as he "expounded the matter to them from morning to evening testifying to the kingdom of God and trying to convince them about Jesus both from the Law of Moses and from the prophets. And some were convinced by what he said, while others disbelieved" (Acts 28:23-24).

This episode was twenty years in the past as Luke wrote. By that time, God's purpose was being carried on in a people composed of Jew and gentile alike, which had been opened to all, but which had, in fact, been rejected by official Judaism. His story thus shows the separation of the *laos* from its Jewish national origins.

Luke's Purpose

Luke's passion story has sometimes been characterized as a personal and parenetic account, one which presents the events as seen through the eyes of a disciple reliving the history of his master.[25] For the disciple, the story of the passion is a summons to follow Jesus on the way of the cross. Luke's intention has been seen as deepening in the disciple his commitment to the following of Jesus, a purpose he achieves partly by painting so many model figures with whom the disciple can identify. Thus the disciple recognizes his own weakness in that of Peter and takes up his cross daily after Jesus, as Simon did. He acknowledges his sinfulness by ranging himself among the crucifiers of Jesus, whose mercy he adores and whose patience he shares.[26] The disciple is thus led to follow Jesus along the trail that he blazed as "leader of life," a trail that leads through suffering to a share in the life of his Risen Lord.

These things are well said. But the details of Luke's crucifixion scene show that his purpose is too narrowly conceived if it is limited to a personal appeal to the individual Christian. The composition of his picture, the presence of the *laos* both as a group and in model or representative figures who incorporate its attitudes, suggest that his picture comes into correct focus only if his intention is recognized as equally ecclesial. Simon of Cyrene is indeed depicted by Luke in the posture of the disciple who takes up his cross to follow Jesus. But Luke shows that Jesus is followed to Calvary by "the whole multitude of the *laos*." The words of Jesus to the women of Jerusalem are a warning addressed not to an individual but to an unfaithful city and people, to an "evil generation."

The Laos at the Cross

With conscious art, Luke surrounds the crucified

Jesus, as he had surrounded the infant Jesus, with the
laos. For Luke, the crucifixion is a climactic step in
the continuing process of division that led to the
emergence of the *laos* which he knew. From the cross,
Jesus speaks for the last time, offering in pardon and
prayer a final revelation of his mission as Messiah and
Son of God to God's people. To the last, he remains
"a sign which is spoken against," bringing to light
the inner dispositions of men, his word acting as the
sword of God's judgment dividing Israel. His claims
are rejected by the leaders of Israel and their minions
and by the unrepentant thief. The *laos* Luke knew
emerges in other figures.

Two figures inside the inner frame exemplify the
main divisions of this *laos*. The repentant thief is
moved by the events of Calvary to a confession of
his sinfulness and acknowledgment of the innocence
of Jesus, as well as to an act of faith in the kingship
of the crucified Christ. He is the first of those who
"call upon the name of the Lord" (Acts 2:21, 9:21;
cf. 4:12, 8:12), who "receive forgiveness of sins in
his name" (Acts 10:43; 22:16). His acceptance of
Jesus as Messiah brings him into the company of
Jesus on the "today" which was Good Friday. By
the words of the crucified, Jesus he is offered "a last
chance of conversion in the last minute,"[27] the same
opportunity as will be offered by the words of the
apostles and accepted by thousands of Jews in Jerusalem in the "today" that is brought about by the
proclamation of the death and resurrection of Jesus.
The centurion, who sees what has happened and responds by glorifying God and confessing Jesus as a
just man, is a forerunner on Calvary of the thousands
of gentiles Luke knew who responded to the preach-

ing of the missioners by glorifying God and acknowl-
edging Jesus as the Righteous One (Acts 10:46; 13:48;
3:14; 7:52).[28]

The two groups into which the *laos* divides after the
crucifixion illustrate the order of the history of salvation in the constitution of the *laos* in the second volume. It is from those who have seen not only the crucifixion but the dead body of Jesus in the finality of
the tomb that the witnesses are chosen. Peter insists
that the Risen Lord was manifested "not to all the
laos but to us who were chosen by God as his witnesses" (Acts 10:39–41). Their eyes opened to discern
the presence of the very Jesus they had seen crucified
and laid in the tomb, and their minds opened to the
message of the Scriptures, they will be able to bring
the crowds to appreciate the divine meaning of the
spectacle they saw but did not understand and thus
lead them from awestruck mourning to conversion and
faith.

The final figure in Luke's gallery serves to remind
his readers that he has been generalizing in his distinction between leaders and *laos*. Like the other three
evangelists, he includes Joseph of Arimathea in the
scene of Jesus' burial. He is a member of the Sanhedrin, but, like Simeon and Anna, a model of Jewish
piety. Joseph is "a member of the Council, a good
and righteous man, who had not consented to their
purpose and deed, and he was awaiting the kingdom
of God" (Lk 23:50). Official Judaism did not reject
Jesus unanimously. Luke knows, and records in Acts,
that in the early years of the Jerusalem community
there were voices in the Sanhedrin like that of Gama-
liel, a man who, though not a believer, was not by
that fact incapable of envisaging the possibility that

"this undertaking is of God," not wishing "to be found resisting God" (Acts 5:38-.39). He knows, too, that the first community was joined by "a great many priests" (Acts 6:7).

Conclusions

By his adaption of the verse in Psalm 22, and the framework it suggests to him, Luke obtains an effect that is unique in the gospel scenes of the crucifixion. Setting *laos* off against the leaders, he makes the crucifixion a climactic step in the process of division that had begun with the ministry of the Baptist, been brought to a head in the ministry of Jesus, and been finalized in the events of Acts. There is still something incomplete, however, in the terms of the antithesis, for if the leaders are portrayed in open rejection of the crucified Christ, the attitude of the *laos,* though not hostile, and even sympathetic, still remains one of incomprehension. On Calvary, the *laos* is depicted in its pre-paschal, pre-pentecostal phase, overcome by events beyond its grasp, until the event of the resurrection and the Spirit-filled proclamation of the witnesses transform it to conversion and faith in the Risen Jesus, Messiah and Lord.

Perhaps we demean Luke's genius when we call it an ability to present theology by tabeaux—at least if theology is conceived as an intellectual exercise. Luke's Calvary scene is no more to be limited to an appeal to the intellect than to an appeal to the individual disciple. His picture is an appeal to the whole *laos* in the whole of its humanity. But once that caveat has been entered, the pictorial quality of the scene, the representative character of its figures, and the significance of their individual attitudes invite a final question. It has been observed that whereas Mark introduces Simon of Cyrene and the women at the cross as witnesses of the events, Luke presents Simon as a model of Christian life and the women as contemplative figures. In this way they recapture, during and after the crucifixion, the attitude of the *laos* at its beginning. But if Simon of Cyrene can be seen as typical of every disciple of Jesus, might not the *laos,* which, when confronted by the crucified Christ "stands by watching," be prototypical of the laos in every age?

It is true that Luke is painting into the scene on Calvary the *laos* whom he is addressing. But there is a condition of the *laos* in every age that may rightly be seen as pre-paschal and pre-pentecostal. Though it certainly experiences the power of the Risen Lord always with it, his presence is always that of a crucified Jesus. So long as their pilgrimage is incomplete, the people of God in each generation are confronted by the mystery of their solidarity with this Christ, and by the essential necessity of suffering if they are to share as a community in the mission of Jesus, Messiah and Son. In this situation, the Risen Lord comes constantly to meet his people through the many ministries by which he enables them to recognize in their painful and humanly incomprehensible experience the presence of one who had to suffer in order to enter into his glory.

He opens their eyes to discern his presence in the many guises in which he joins them "on the way," and opens minds and hearts to the lesson of the Scriptures. Through the witness of Christian lives, human suffering becomes credible as a solidarity with the crucified Christ. The proclamation of this crucified Christ as Risen Lord continues to convert incomprehension into faith, and the "breaking of the bread" of the Eucharist proclaims his death and offers to his people their clearest glimpse of his face, until he comes.

Notes

1. Cf. A. Rose, "L'influence des Psaumes sur les annonces et les récits de la Passion et de la Résurrection dans les Evangiles," *Le Psautier,* ed. R. DeLanghe (Louvain, 1962), pp. 316f.

3. For a treatment of the apostles' "standing by" Jesus in the Lucan passion narrative, cf. S. Brown, *Apostasy and Perseverance in the Theology of Luke* (Rome, 1969), pp. 66-70. J. C. Hawkins, *Horae Synopticae* (2d ed.; Oxford, 1909), p. 196, lists Lk 23:48 among the "smaller additions in St. Luke's Gospel to which the other Synoptics have no parallels" and classes them as additions which merely heighten the effect of the narrative. But a closer examination of the texts he cites under that rubric shows that many of these texts serve precisely as vehicles for Luke's theology.

4. For the significance of these events, cf. G. Stahlin, *Theological Dictionary of the New Testament,* ed. G. Kittel (Grand Rapids, Mich., 1964), 3:830-60; A. Stoger, *The Gospel according to St. Luke* (New York, 1969), 2:232.

5. If this analysis is correct, it spoils the neat division of vv. 33-49 into four parts, built on a schema of three each, proposed by W. Grundmann in *Das Evangelium nach Lukas* (Berlin, 1966), p. 431. It should be remarked that the prayer of Jesus in v. 34 falls outside this inner frame.

6. On the subject of the *laos,* cf. H. Strathmann, *Theological Dictionary of the New Testament,* 4:50-57, though it is to be noted that the original fascicle was written in 1938 and some of his conclusions call for revisions. See also H. Conzelmann, *The Theology of Saint Luke* (New York, 1960), pp. 163f.; J. Jervell, *Luke and the*

People of God (Minneapolis, 1972), pp. 41-74; J. Kodell, "Luke's Use of *Laos* 'People' Especially in the Jerusalem Narrative," *Catholic Biblical Quarterly* 31 (1969): 327-43. Both Kodell and J. Fitzmyer ("Anti-Semitism and the Cry of 'All the People,'" *Theological Studies* 26 [1965]:669) regard the term *laos* in Luke as a generic term often equaling *ochlos*. Not all of Kodell's instances are probative, and the more modified judgment of A. George ("Israel dans l'oeuvre de Luc", *Rêvue Biblique* 75 [1968]: 482, n. 4) is followed here.

7. Cf. L. Legrand, "L'Evangile aux Bergers. Essai sur le genre littéraire de Luc II:8-20," *Rêvue Biblique* 75 (1968): 161-87.

8. Cf. P. Minear, "Luke's Use of the Infancy Stories," *Studies in Luke-Acts,* ed. Keck-Martyn (New York, 1966), pp. 111-31.

9. Zeph 3:14-17; Joel 2:21-27; Zech 9:9-10.

10. Cf. A. George, "La royauté de Jésus selon l'évangile de Luc," *Sciences Ecclesiastiques* 14 (1962): 57-69; idem, "Jesus fils de Dieu dans l'évangile selon saint Luc," *Revue Biblique* 72 (1965):195-209; L. Legrand, "L'arriére-plan néo-testamentaire de Luc 1:35," *Revue Bibblique* 70 (1963):161-92.

11. P. Benoit, "Et toi-même, un glaive te transpercera l'âme," *Catholic Biblical Quarterly* 25 (1963):251-61; A. Feuillet, "L'épreuve prédite à Marie par le vicillard Siméon," *A la Recontre de Dieu* (Le Puy, 1961), pp. 243-64.

12. Cf. B. M. F. van Iersel, "The Finding of Jesus in the Temple," *Novum Testamentum* 4 (1960):161-73.

13. Cf. Conzelmann, *Theology of St. Luke,* p. 164.

14. Isaiah 40:3 is utilized in different ways in Mt 3:3; Mk 1:2-3; Jn 1:23. Luke continues the citation to include Is 40:3-5.

15. Cf. H. Flendor, *St. Luke, Theologian of Redemptive History* (London, 1967), pp. 74-75.

16. On the question of Jesus' audiences, cf. A. W. Mosley, "Jesus' Audiences in the Gospels of St. Mark and St. Luke," *New Testament Studies* 10 (1963/64):139-149 and the computerized treatment of J. A. Baird, *Audience Criticism and the Historical Jesus* (Philadelphia, 1969).

17. On this section especially, cf. Kodell, "Luke's Use of Laos," pp. 327-32.

18. Cf. Flender, *St. Luke,* pp. 107-9; P. Simson, "The Drama of

the City of God in St. Luke's Gospel," *Scripture* 15 (1963):65-80.

19. Cf. Kodell, "Luke's Use of *Laos,*" pp. 328ff., for a detailed discussion of these episodes and for the possibly discordant uses of *laos* in Lk 21:23 and especially in Lk 23:13.

20. Cf. George, "Israel dans l'oeuvre de Luc," p. 501. B. S. Easton, *The Gospel According to St. Luke* (New York, 1926), judged v. 38 as "something of an anti-climax." V. Taylor, *The Passion Narrative of St. Luke* (Cambridge, 1972), p. 93, sees the verse as "an after-thought suggested by the soldier's taunt," interrupting a deliberately constructed sequence. On the contrary, Luke has reserved it for this point to heighten the impression of ignominy.

21. Cf. P. Benoit, *The Passion and Resurrection of Jesus Christ* (New York, 1969), p. 179.

22. Luke uses serveral compounds of the verb *strephein* ("turn") in his vocabulary of penance, but never *hypostrephein,* the word used of the return of the crowds (23:48) and of the women (23:58). The special emphasis on penance in the post-pentecostal period is remarked on by G. W. H. Lampe in "The Holy Spirit in the Writings of St. Luke," *Studies in the Gospels,* ed. D. H. Nineham (Oxford, 1955), pp. 186f.

23. Cf. also Acts 10:39, 13:27, and J. Dupont, "Repentir et conversion selon les Actes des Apotres," *Etudes sur les Actes des Apôtres* (Paris, 1967), pp. 47-50.

24. The meaning of the phrase has been established by N. A. Dahl in "A People for His Name (Acts 15:14)," *New Testament Studies* 4 (1957):319-27.

25. For recent treatments of the death of Jesus in the theology of Luke, cf. Grundmann, *Das Evangelium mach Lukas,* pp. 454-57, and especially the careful analysis of George, "Le sens de la mort de Jesus pour Luc," *Revue Biblique* 80 (1973):186-217.

26. Cf. X. Leon-Dufour, "Passion, Recits de la," *Dictionnaire de la Bible,* Supplement (7 vols.; Paris, 1928-), 6:1477.

27. Cf. Grundmann, *Das Evangelium nach Lukas,* p. 432.

28. Ibid., p. 435. For another view, cf. G. D. Kilpatrick, "A Theme of the Lucan Passion Story and Luke 23:47," *Journal of Theological Studies* 43 (1942):34-36.

The Death of Jesus
as Revelation
in John's Gospel

Aelred Lacomara C.P.
Saint John's University
Jamaica, New York

To say that the theology of the fourth gospel is a theology of incarnation is a commonplace. And rightly so, for the key to the thought of John is certainly in the fact that "the Word became flesh and made his dwelling among us" (Jn 1:14). It is in Jesus' humanity, acting among men in a genuinely human way, that there is seen that revelation which Jesus brings, with which, in fact, he is identified. What is expressed in his manhood is the living, loving presence of God in the world, "the glory of an only Son coming from the Father, filled with enduring love" (Jn 1:14). The whole gospel could be considered an exposition of this verse.

But it would be a mistake to say, as some have, that John expresses a theology of incarnation as opposed, for example, to a Pauline theology of death and resurrection. As we hope to show in this essay, a theology of the death of Jesus is central in John's thought. It is a theme that runs through the entire gospel, not in addition to that of incarnation, but as its necessary complement. For John, the cross is the ultimate completion of the mission of Jesus, as it is the ultimate act of his humanity. By it, the true identity of Jesus and the nature of his ministry are revealed, and his work finally accomplished. As C. H. Dodd has written, "If in the incarnate life of Christ the eternal, archetypal light is manifested, its final manifestation is in His death."[1] It would surely be too

105

much to say of John, as has been said of Mark, that it is a passion narrative with a long introduction. Still, John has this in common with the synoptic gospels, and indeed with the whole of early Christian thought, that the cross of Jesus is the ultimate revelation of God in Christ.

Portents of the Passion

From the earliest verses of the fourth gospel, intimations of the passion are prominent. Even in the prologue, the conflict between the revelatory Word of God and those to whom he is sent is seen as inevitable. And though "the light shines on in the darkness" (Jn 1:5), the darkness is unrelenting in its efforts to overcome it. The majority of scholars hold that this verse refers not to the earthly ministry of Jesus but to the primeval struggle between good and evil that is narrated in Genesis. But the incarnation of the Word certainly neither interrupts the conflict nor changes its essential nature. This is clear in Jn 1:10, where, by way of forecast, we are told that the world refused to recognize the revelation of God in Jesus and that his own people rejected him. It has been argued that this verse, too, speaks of the career of the Word before he became flesh. There is not space here to discuss the question,[2] but even if the theory should be accepted that the verse's reference is to the coming of the Word to the world and to Israel through law and wisdom, it still reinforces the ineluctability of conflict and rejection when the Word appears in human history, finally and definitively, in the manhood of Jesus.

With the first public appearance of Jesus in the fourth gospel, this conclusion becomes inescapable. He is immediately identified by the Baptist as the "Lamb of God" (Jn 1:29, 36). True, a series of titles is attributed to Jesus in Jn 1, but greater significance attaches to the identification by the Baptist than to any other, for in the fourth gospel the Baptist has a special function as the spokesman for the evangelist. It is only the Baptist, for example, who knows Jesus as the bearer and giver of the Spirit and as the Chosen One of God (Jn 1:32-34). And if Jn 3:31-36 be accepted—at least in the text as we have it—as the words of the Baptist, then it is he who knows of the intimate relationship between Jesus and the Father. On his lips, therefore, the identification of Jesus as Lamb of God assumes particular importance, since it indicates the intention of the evangelist to see the whole ministry of Jesus in light of this title.

What does the title tell us about Jesus and his ministry? Against the background of the Old Testament, the term immediately calls to mind the image of the paschal lamb, by whose blood the Israelites had been signed for preservation from the last plague in Egypt, which was therefore considered in Jewish thought to have been instrumental in liberating the people from bondage. In the early Christian community the death of Jesus had been compared to the paschal sacrifice, and the imagery was in common use before the fourth gospel was written (cf. 1 Cor 5:7; 1 Pet 1:18f.). John himself uses the imagery in his account of the crucifixion (e.g., Jn 19:36). It is clear, therefore, that by "Lamb of God" we are to understand that Jesus is destined for sacrifice, and by his blood the people will be freed from bondage—in this case, as the gospel makes clear, from the bondage of sin (cf. Jn 8:34-36).

There is, of course, another use of lamb imagery in

the Old Testament that throws light on the meaning
of its application to Jesus. Is 53:7 describes the suffering servant as one who is "led to the slaughter like a
sheep, and like a lamb before its shearers." The mere
use of the same imagery would hardly prove that the
evangelist had the suffering servant in mind in the passage we are considering. But the same passage also
describes Jesus as the one on whom the Spirit rests,
and designates him as "God's Chosen One," and it is
in these same terms that the servant is described in Is
42:1 and 41:1. Jesus is thus presented as the one who
fulfills the role of the servant in bearing the sins of
the world and achieving his own glorification and the
justification of the people.[3] This interpretation is con-
firmed by the very explicit reference to the servant
in Jn 12:38 (cf. Is 53:1). Once again, therefore, we
can say that the Baptist's proclamation of Jesus points
to his eventual death for the salvation of the people.
This will be the culmination as well as the end of his
mission.

The indications of the importance of Jesus' suffering and death in the theology of John continue throughout the gospel. Jn 3:14, for example, speaks of Jesus'
being "lifted up" and, indeed, of the *necessity* of it for
his mission. There is more intended in this phrase than
a general comparison to the serpent lifted up by Moses
in the desert. Jesus again uses the phrase of himself in
Jn 12:32, and the evangelist states clearly in the following verse: "This statement indicated the sort of death
he had to die." Again, we note the element of necessity in the death of Jesus. There can be no doubt that
the "lifting up" refers primarily to the crucifixion, both
in these verses and in its use by Jesus in his contro-
versy with the Jews in Jn 8:28. As we shall see, these

are key verses in understanding the revelatory character of Jesus' death.

John's choice of the expression "lifting up" to describe the death of Jesus is also indicative of this theology that the death was not only a physical raising of the incarnate Word on a cross, but the first stage of his ultimate glorification in resurrection and ascension to the Father. It is quite probable that the evangelist adopted the phrase from Is 52:13, where it is said of the servant that God will "lift him up and glorify him exceedingly." Again, servant theology is apparent as applied to Jesus and runs as a motif through the gospel. On the very eve of the crucifixion Jesus presents himself as a servant in washing the feet of his disciples (Jn 13:3-12), a symbolic forecast of the work he was to accomplish on the following day.[4]

The necessity of Jesus' death, so prominent in the above verses, is a clear indication that John sees it as an essential part of God's plan of salvation and hence totally under divine control. Further indication of this is in the frequent reference to Jesus' death and glorification as his "hour," a point in time that cannot come until the Father wills it (Jn 2:4, 7:30, 8:20; and cf. 7:6-8). That the "hour" refers to the death of Jesus is clear in Jn 12:23, 27, where it is the time of Jesus' glorification and hence of his death, and in Jn 13:1, where it is the time assigned for Jesus to pass to the Father. That the "hour has come" is the first phrase Jesus addresses to his Father in the prayer by which he consecrates himself to his approaching sacrifice (Jn 17:1). The repetition of the hour theme through the gospel has the dramatic effect of continually drawing the attention of the reader forward to the final Passover of Jesus' life, to the events that will be the final revelation of the meaning of Jesus and his ministry.

This dramatic effect is enhanced by John's characteristic device of introducing deliberate misunderstanding into Jesus' discourses. Constantly, Jesus speaks on one level but is understood—or misunderstood—on a different level. It becomes increasingly clear that the misunderstandings will require a truly climactic event for their resolution, and this is found only in the death and concomitant glorification of Jesus (cf., e.g., Jn 2:22, 8:28, 13:7). The events of the ministry continue to look to the death of Jesus for their ultimate meaning.

The Cross and the Revelation of Jesus

The verses we have considered as portents of the crucifixion make it clear that, for John, Jesus' death will have a revelatory character. This is particularly apparent in the verses that speak of the "lifting up." In each of these verses Jesus applies to himself the title "Son of Man," with the clear implication that it is precisely under this title that he goes to his death.[5] The context of Jn 3:14 shows the appropriateness of this. In verse 13 the Son of Man is the one who is uniquely qualified to mediate between heaven and earth; he is the "connecting link between the earthly and heavenly spheres; his earthly existence is the place where heavenly things become visible, and also the place where heavenly things are rejected by mankind."[6] The ultimate rejection was the cross. As the mediator who comes from heaven, Jesus reveals to men the knowledge and love of God which constitute the true and eternal life of mankind. He does this not as some ethereal heavenly being but as man, in the fullness of his humanity. His death becomes his ultimate descent into the human condition, and thus his ultimate revelation of himself as a true "son of man." Paradoxically, it is this culminating act of his descent that is identifcal with his glorification, for his lifting up into death is his passage to the Father and the exaltation of his humanity, the showing forth of what genuine humanity is intended by God to be. Thus if it is in his humanity that Jesus is the revelation of God, then it is in the culminating human act of dying that the revelation is complete.

The death of Jesus is shown as under the control of the Father in the divine plan of salvation. But the agency of men is not overlooked. Jn 8:28 has Jesus saying to his enemies that it is *they* who will lift up the Son of Man. It will be their final rejection of the revelation which Jesus is. But here, too, there is a paradox. By their rejection of Jesus and their lifting him up in crucifixion, they bring the revelation which they have rejected to its completion. And their rejection is not, at base, a judgment which they make on the authenticity of Jesus as revelation. On the contrary, that revelation passes judgment on them (Jn 3:17-21), for Jesus, and especially in the brutally human act of his death, it demands a response, a response that is necessarily a self-judgment of the man who makes it. For the fourth gospel, it is in this way that the Son of Man, in his lifting up, fulfills the role traditionally associated with that title, that of bringing judgment on the world.[7]

The rejection of the Son of Man does not, therefore, hinder God's plan of salvation; it furthers it. This is expressed in Jn 12:23f., 32. It is by the lifting up, the glorification, of the Son of Man that his work of redemption is brought to fruition and that men are drawn to him. His ultimate act of self-revelation proves irresistible to those who are willing to "keep faith in the light" (Jn 12:36).

The messiahship, too, of the Son of Man is revealed in his death, or, more precisely, in his conquest of death. John establishes this, in the first place, by the close connection he makes between the raising of Lazarus and the acclamation of Jesus as king. In the account of Jesus' triumphal entry into Jerusalem on Palm Sunday, he is hailed with the words "Blessed is the King of Israel" (Jn 12:13). John makes it clear that the actions of the crowd are a direct result of the testimony of those who had seen Jesus conquer death in the raising of Lazarus (Jn 12:17-18). This leads to his recognition as king. This same theme is continued in the passion narrative itself, where the kingship of Jesus is a prominent motif. On the surface, of course, the sufferings of Jesus make a mockery of his kingship (Jn 19:1-3), and his claim is rejected in explicit terms by the people (Jn 19:14-1 6). Nevertheless, the legitimacy of the claim and the true nature of his kingship are maintained in the dialogue with Pilate in Jn 18:33-38. Jesus is Messiah in that he saves those who will receive his testimony to the truth of God. His rejection does not nullify his kingship. On the contrary, it is by going to the cross that he conquers death, once for all, and bears the ultimate witness in which his kingship consists. It is precisely on the cross that he can most completely be exhibited as the "King of the Jews" (Jn 19:19).

By telling us that the written proclamation of Jesus' kingship was in three well-known languages, John may intend to convey that this kingship was universalized at Jesus' death. Whether that is the intention of this verse, there is no doubt that it is the teaching of John. The Pharisees intimate this when Jesus is first hailed on Palm Sunday: "See, there is nothing you can do! The whole world has run after him" (Jn 12:19). And when, in Jn 12:20-22, gentile Greeks approach Jesus, he recognizes that the hour of his glorification has arrived. With his death, his lordship is extended to all mankind. His crucifixion will be an invitation to all men to accept the divine truth to which he attests and thus to accept his kingship. Jesus himself asserts this when he says that in his glorification the evil that has held sway in the world—the "prince of this world"—is cast out. Lordship belongs to Jesus alone, and to him precisely as crucified: "And I, once I am lifted up from the earth, will draw all men to myself" (Jn 12:31-32).

This claim to lordship, actualized on the cross, is also phrased by John in a striking way when he has Jesus apply to himself the words "I am." These words, used absolutely and, as it were, as a title for Jesus, are found four times in the gospel (Jn 8:24, 28, 58; 13:19).[8] The background for this absolute use of the phrase is to be found in the Greek version of the Old Testament, where it is used by God of himself.[9] Its most probable meaning is its reference to the uniqueness and unchangeableness of God, with at least an allusion to the divine name "Yahweh." In John, therefore, Jesus claims for himself eternal being that places him on a level with God. It is no less than a claim to divinity.[10] And it is the truth of this claim that Jesus says will be recognized in his glorification through death: "When you lift up the Son of Man, you will come to realize that I am" (Jn 8:28). The Johannine paradox appears again: it is at the most human moment of his death that Jesus will be revealed as divine.

The relationship of Jesus to the Father is thus a revelation from the cross. Once more, John makes this explicit when he notes that the claim to be God's Son was one of the charges that led to Jesus' death, and a charge that had a profound effect on Pilate (Jn 19:7f.). For the Jews, it was the principal "crime" for which Jesus deserved death (Jn 19:7). Earlier, they had determined on his death for the very reason that he "was speaking of God as his own Father, thereby making himself God's equal" (Jn 5:18). And they were ready to carry out their resolve by stoning him for his claim (Jn 10:33, 36). They could not succeed because his hour had not come. But when it came, he was condemned for his claim to divine sonship. "It is as the Son that Jesus goes to the cross."[11]

Relationship of Love

At its most fundamental, the revelation of the cross is the divine disclosure of the relationships of love between the Father and the Son, and between God and man. For John, as for the entire New Testament, the crucifixion of Jesus finds its reason in the love of God bestowed on the world in Jesus, and reciprocated first by Jesus and then, in Jesus, by those who believe in him. The classic text for the expression of the divine love is Jn 3:16: "Yes, God so loved the world that he gave his only Son, that whoever believes in him may not die but may have eternal life." Here is no general speculation on divine love but a historical reference to a very concrete expression of that love. This expression is found, certainly, in the incarnation itself. But the context of the verse, especially verse 14, with its reference to the "lifting up" of Jesus, indicates that it is the death and glorification of Jesus that is specifically meant. It is in this, preeminently, that God's love for the world is expressed, and hence revealed. This interpretation of the verse receives further support from the fact that the verb "gave" becomes almost a technical term in the New Testament for the act by which the Father hands over the Son to redemptive death.[12]

Again, the universality of the love, and of the effectiveness of its expression in the death of Jesus, is strongly to the fore. It is nothing less than the entire world that God loves and to which he offers eternal life in the death of Jesus. But the love is not forced. We are once more reminded that it benefits only those who receive Jesus in faith.[13] And once more we find the Johannine paradox: the glorious revelation of God's love is veiled in the self-abasement of Jesus' mode of death, which, for John, is itself the act of glorification.[14] Acceptance in faith is necessary for the veil to be pierced, for the glory to be revealed. "For only the man who overcomes the offense of Jesus' humility, and who perceives his exaltation in his death, can see in Jesus the Son sent by the Father."[15] And only the man who sees this can apprehend the love of God that the cross reveals.

In his love for Jesus, the Father reveals to him the intimate secrets of divinity. "For the Father loves the Son and everything the Father does he shows him" (Jn 5:20). This, of course, would include the divine plan of salvation and Jesus' place in it. Jesus' response to this plan, especially as it concerns himself, constitutes his return of love to his Father. "Yes, I know him well," Jesus says, "and I keep his word" (Jn 8:55). John expresses this response of love by emphasizing that

Jesus goes to his death with full knowledge and purpose (cf. Jn 6:64, 70f.; 13:11, 21-27). In turn, this conformity of Jesus to the Father's will in his death is given as a particular reason for the Father's love for Jesus: "The Father loves me for this, that I lay down my life to take it up again. No one takes it from me; I lay it down freely . . . This command I received from my Father" (Jn 10:17-18). It is in this spirit of mutual love that Jesus accepts the cup the Father has prepared for him (Jn 18:11) and freely goes to the hour of his death (Jn 12:27-28). Jn 14:31 is, surprisingly, the only passage in the fourth gospel in which this love of Jesus for the Father is mentioned in explicit terms: "the world must know that I love the Father and do as he has commanded me." Coming as a climax in Jesus' farewell discourse to his disciples, the reference can only be to his imminent crucifixion. It is quite evident in this verse that Jesus considers what he is about to do as revelatory of his love, since by his death the world will see the evidence of that love.

But it is not alone out of love for the Father that Jesus goes willingly to his death. It is for love of man as well. This theme appears several times in the gospel. In Jn 10:11 Jesus speaks of himself in the beautiful imagery of the good shepherd who "lays down his life for the sheep." We should note that in the Old Testament this shepherd imagery is used of God himself.[16] Jesus assumes the divine task of shepherding the sheep, to the point of giving his life for them, thus proving his fidelity and love. This relationship between Jesus and his flock is a reflection of the relationship between Jesus and his Father (Jn 10:14-15), and it is the same intensity of love that motivates his sacrifice for them. The universality of that love and the effectiveness of the sacrifice are again made explicit in the reference to the "other sheep" who are brought into the "one fold" (Jn 10:16). As we shall see, the formation of a salvation community is the object of Jesus' mission and the means of continuing the revelation of the cross.

That Jesus dies for the people is a theme that is expressed even by his enemies. In Jn 11:50-52 the high priest Caiaphas makes his decision that it is better for "one man to die than to have the whole nation perish." For John, the meaning of this statement goes beyond the sophistry of political expediency. He sees in the words of the high priest a prophecy, and therefore a word of God, that Jesus' death would be for the benefit of the nation and, indeed, for a universal gathering of all God's children into unity (Jn 11:51-52).[17] Again, emphasis is placed on the formation of a community as a purpose of Jesus' death. That John saw a special importance in Caiaphas' prophecy is evident from the fact that he refers to it again in the passion narrative in Jn 18:14.

The motif of Jesus' death for the sake of the people is again expressed on the eve of that death in his high-priestly prayer, and expressed in terms that reveal even more about the nature of his death. In Jn 17:19 Jesus says of himself and his disciples: "I consecrate myself for their sakes now, that they may be consecrated in truth." The Old Testament uses the term "consecrate" for the act of setting something or someone aside for divine service. The term is used in a particular sense for the preparation of a priest or of a victim for sacrifice (cf. Ex 13:2, 28:41, Dt 15:19). It is most probably in this sense that Jesus uses the word in his final prayer.[18] This is indicated by the position of the prayer immediately before the passion narrative, in which John will use symbolism to designate Jesus as both priest and victim. We may recall that Jesus has already been identified as a sacrificial victim with the title "Lamb of God." The present passage functions, then, as his "offertory prayer," in which, as priestly mediator between God and man, he offers himself to the Father for the same purpose for which any sacrifice is offered, that man may find union with God.

For the disciples, the immediate effect of this union will be to fit them for their apostolic mission. This mission will be to bring others into that same union which the sacrifice of Jesus makes possible. Hence they, too, can be said to be "consecrated" with the consecration of Jesus, just as their sending is the continuation of the Father's sending of Jesus into the world (Jn 17:16-17). Again, the purpose of the sacrifice, as of the sending, is the formation of a community of faith and love, a union of man with God and with one another in Jesus (Jn 17:20-23a). It is in the life of this community that the revelation of the cross finds a continuing concrete expression and thus manifests its message to the world: the nature of God, the divine love that is seen in the work of Jesus, and the fulfillment of human life that his work offers to man (Jn 17:23b, 25-26). "This [love] is the ultimate mystery of Godhead which Jesus revealed to the world . . . The love of God, thus released in history, brings men into the same unity of which the relation of Father and Son is the eternal archetype."[19]

The Crucifixion Scene

The rich symbolism that John has worked into his account of the death of Jesus has been noted and analyzed by many scholars. Not as often noticed, however, is the way in which this symbolism brings together and illustrates the· theology of Jesus' death, which is, as we have seen, woven in several strands through the preceding sections of the gospel. Paschal imagery, for example, is highlighted by the fact that Jesus goes to his death, as John tells us with unusual precision, on the very day and hour that the paschal lambs were being sacrificed (Jn 19:14)—as well as in the reference to hyssop (19:29; cf. Ex 12:22) and in the application to Jesus of an Old Testament passage that specifically refers to the sacrificed lambs (Jn 19: 36; cf. Ex 12:46). With characteristic irony, then, John has the priests calling for the death of the Lamb of God that will initiate the New Covenant at the moment when others of their number are solicitously sacrificing the paschal lambs of the Old Covenant. All unknowing, they bring to fulfillment the deliverance which the original Exodus forecast.

Similarly, and again without knowing the full significance of the action, the gentile Pilate insists on affixing the title "King of the Jews" to the cross against the objections of the Jewish leaders, who have claimed Caesar as their only king (Jn 19:19-22). The theme of the universality of Jesus' lordship in his death is thus underscored again, as is the theme of division and judgment which the scandal of the cross provokes. This same lordship is evident in the fact that Jesus, contrary to the tradition in the synoptic gospels, carries his cross alone (19:17). In the thought of John, it must be made explicit that the entire work of re-

demption is in the control of Jesus from beginning to
end. Thus it was only by his consent that he was ar-
rested (Jn 18:1-12), and it is by his own deliberate
act that "he bowed his head" in death (Jn 19:30).
Here we are reminded once more of the perfect freedom in love with which the Son does the will of his
Father.

Jesus' prayer in Jn 17 made reference to the priestly
aspect of his self-offering. This aspect is brought to
the fore in the crucifixion scene by the reference to the
seamless tunic for which the executioners gamble (Jn
19:23-24). It can scarcely be doubted that in this in-
cident John would have us think of the robe of the
high priest as it is described in Ex 28:4, 29:5, 39:27,
and Lev 16:4. Thus, at the moment of his execution,
Jesus is seen in the priestly role of sacrificer and mediator, for which both his humanity and his relationship to the Father make him uniquely qualified. For
John, the death of Jesus is an act of sacrifice which
brings God and man together in a unity of life.[20]
Such a unity must, of course, unite believers in a unity
among themselves, and this fact has also been seen in
the symbolism of the undivided robe. If this is, in
fact, a secondary interpretation of the symbol, it is,
of course, quite appropriate to John's theme.

The theme of a community of life continues through
the events of the crucifixion scene and is quite prominent in Jesus' giving his mother to the "beloved
disciple" (Jn 19:26-27). This disciple stands by the
cross, not only in his own person, but as representative of all the faithful followers of Jesus. Similarly,
the mother of Jesus also plays a symbolic role.[21] This
is apparent in Jesus' addressing her as "woman," a
title that was not a customary address of a son to

his mother but that is certainly evocative of the woman of Gen 3:20, the "mother of all the living," and
of the Old Testament's description of Israel as a woman
who, after her desolation, becomes the mother of many
children from all the nations (cf. Is 49:20-22; 54:1;
66:7-14). This symbolism is used earlier by John (in
16:21-22) to describe the disciples of Jesus as being,
at his death, like a woman suffering the pangs of
labor but ultimately rejoicing at the birth of new life.
Very similar is the Johannine imagery of Rev 12:1-6,
17, where the "woman" (the new Israel) brings forth
the Messiah in pain and has other offspring who are
characterized as those who "keep God's command-
ments and give witness to Jesus" (cf. Jn 15:14, 27).
It seems evident, then, that in Jn 19:26-27 the mother of Jesus, as "new Eve" and "new Israel," is the
figure of that community of faith and love through
which the individual disciples will find the gift of spirit and life which is the legacy of the crucified Lord.
Thus is the promised sheepfold of the shepherd established, and a new people brought into being, by
his death.

With the founding of a community that will bear
continuing witness to him and to his word, the work
of Jesus is accomplished (Jn 19:28). The fourth gospel
has repeatedly stressed the freedom and complete will-
ingness with which Jesus obeys his Father's command.
This theme occurs again in Jn 19:28, where, in the
words "I thirst," dramatic emphasis is given to Jesus'
desire to fulfill to the letter the Father's plan of salvation as it was outlined in the Old Testament. More
than likely, the thirst, and the common wine in verse
29, refer to the fulfillment of Pss 22:16 and 69:22. But
in the context of so much Johannine symbolism, the

thought of John goes beyond a simple, literal fulfillment of texts, and the thirst of Jesus can be seen as
an intense desire to drink to the very dregs of death
the cup which his Father has given him (Jn 18:11).
Johannine irony is detected once more: a deathly
thirst afflicts Jesus at the very moment that his going
to the Father makes him the source of living water.
In a brief text, John again expresses the relationship
of love between Jesus and the Father, and between
Jesus and man.

The same relationships are expressed, with equal
terseness, in John's description of Jesus' death: "And
bowing his head, he handed over his spirit" (Jn 19:30).
In this verse John seems to follow the same tradition
as Mt 27:50 and Lk 23:46 in seeing the death of
Jesus as a surrender of his life (spirit) into the hands
of his Father. Certainly the words mean more than
the simple fact that Jesus dies, for "handing over the
spirit," as a phrase meaning "to die," is as awkward
in Greek as it is in English. John thus brings to a
conclusion the theme of Jesus' complete self-surrender
to the will of his Father, even—and especially—in the
act of dying. Jesus' priestly offering of himself as victim, announced in Jn 17:19, is accomplished.

But, as so often in the fourth gospel, the words of
Jn 19:30 have a twofold meaning. If the handing
over of the spirit is Jesus' giving of his life to the
Father, it is also the giving of his promised Spirit
to his disciples. It is thus in context with the other
episodes of the crucifixion scene, where the actions and
words of Jesus are related both to God and to man
and point to the establishment of the Christian community. For it is only by the giving of the Spirit of
Jesus that the community finds its unity and life. It

is true that John narrates the giving of the Spirit only after the resurrection (Jn 20:22), but he symbolically anticipates that post-resurrection act and connects it intimately with the death of Jesus in order to show as vividly as possible that the giving of the Spirit is the fruit of that death. This accords with Jn 7:39, where we were told that the Spirit could be sent only after Jesus had been glorified, and with Jn 16:7, where Jesus declares the necessity of his "going" for the Spirit to be sent. For John, the "going" of Jesus and the essential moment of his glorification are his death.

The death of Jesus, then, not only brings his mission from the Father to a climax, it ensures that the mission will continue in his disciples. With them, now, is the Spirit who rested on Jesus at the beginning of his ministry (Jn 1:31-34) and who will be for them the principle of a new life (Jn 3:5-8), of the new worship which the death of Jesus inaugurates (Jn 4:24), of the continuing revelation of the depths of Jesus' message (Jn 16:12-15), and hence of the continuing witness to Jesus' presence in the world (Jn 15:26-27). The revelation that came in Jesus, the revelation that *is* Jesus, and which reached its climax on the cross, thus lives on in his disciples through the Spirit whom his death communicates.

This same theme is continued by John in his graphic account of the piercing of Jesus' side after his death. John attaches deep significance to this episode and underscores its importance by his insistence that its truth is guaranteed by eyewitness testimony (Jn 19:34-35). Whatever may be the historical or physiological fact in the flow of blood and water from Jesus' side, its theological significance for John can be determined from its context and from prior passages in the gospel. Jn 4:10, 14 speaks of Jesus as the source of the living water of eternal life. This imagery recurs in Jn 7:37-38, where, as we have seen, the living water is interpreted as the Spirit. In the present passage, then, John reiterates his teaching that with the death of Jesus the Spirit of life is given. For this reason, the flow of water is commingled with that of blood, the symbol of death; the sending of the Spirit is inseparable from the death of Jesus.

Through the centuries, many commentators have seen in the water and blood a reference to the sacraments of baptism and the Eucharist. This interpretation is certainly plausible since Jn 3:5 has used water to refer to baptism, and Jn 6:53-56 speaks of the eucharistic blood of Jesus. Both are considered sources of life. In the context of the crucifixion scene, of course, where the theme of the founding of a community is so prominent, such sacramental symbolism would be quite in place, since it is by baptism that one is born into the Christian community and by the Eucharist that the life of that community is sustained. If this interpretation reflects John's meaning, then he is saying yet again that Jesus' death is the source of the authentic life of men. But he is again quick to remind us that this life comes only to those who, in *faith*, "look on him whom they have pierced" (Jn 19:37).

Jesus himself summed up the purpose of his entire mission as the ultimate revelation of God and of the divine love, and the incorporation of men into this love by their union with Jesus and with one another: "To them I have revealed your name, and I will continue to reveal it so that your love for me may live in them, and I may live in them" (Jn 17:26).

This revelation is the finality of the incarnation, and its ultimate act is the crucifixion. The love of God for the world, as we have seen, is manifested in his giving of his only Son, even in death. And the responsive love of the Son is shown in his acceptance of the Father's command by laying down hi life for his friends (cf. Jn 15:13).

But the prominence in the crucifixion scene of the idea of founding a community makes it obvious that the dying of Jesus is not only a momentary exhibition of this revelation of love. It is, like Jesus himself, a living reality that is to continue in the world in the witness of those who follow him. The Spirit of truth—who is also the Spirit of life and love—is the authenticating bond between the mission of Jesus and that of his disciples (cf. Jn 15:26-27, 20:21-22). As the Father has given a commandment of love to Jesus, so has Jesus given a commandment of mutual love to his followers, who, in their oneness with him, are his friends (cf. Jn 13:34, 15:12-15). The response of Jesus to the Father's love, the cross, is the exemplar of the disciples' response to the command of Jesus. Their mutual love is thus a reflection of the mutual and eternal love that exists between Father and Son. It is the revelation of the incarnate Word living on in the world. And as Jesus found the ultimate in human freedom and fulfillment in his obedience to the Father, so do the disciples in obedience to him. For the fourth gospel, this is the word of the cross.

Notes

1. *The Interpretation of the Fourth Gospel* (Cambridge, 1958), p. 208.

2. The main points of the varying interpretations are given in R. E. Brown, *The Gospel According to John, I-XII* (Anchor Bible, 29) (Garden City, N.Y., 1966), pp. 28-30.

3. For a full discussion of these verses as indicative of servant theology, cf. T. Stanks, *The Servant of God in Jn 1:29, 36* (Louvain, 1963). A short but adequate discussion is in C. K. Barrett, *The Gospel According to John* (London, 1958), pp. 146-47.

4. For the "servant" interpretation of the foot washing, cf. Brown, *The Gospel According to John, XIII-XXI* (Anchor Bible, 29 A) (Garden City, N.Y., 1970), pp. 558-68.

5. The same is true of the passion predictions in Mk 8:31, 9:31, and 10:33 (cf. the parallels in Mt. and Lk), to which the three "lifting up" passages in Jn correspond.

6. Barrett, *John*, p. 177.

7. Cf. R. Schnackenburg, *The Gospel According to St. John* (New York, 1968), 1:531-32.

8. For a brief but lucid analysis of this usage in Jn, cf. Brown, *John I-XII*, pp. 533-38.

9. For a parallel to Jn 8:24, for example, cf. Is 43:10.

10. Cf. Barrett, *John*, p. 283.

11. G. Delling, *Der Kreuzestod Jesu in der urchristlichen Verkündigung* (Gottingen, 1972), p. 103.

12. For close parallels to Jn 3:16, cf. another Johannine writing, 1 Jn 4:9, and in the Pauline writings, Gal 4:4 and Rom 8:3. A good analysis of these verses and their bearing on a theology of the passion is found in Delling, *Kreuzestod*, pp. 104-5.

13. Cf. T. Barrosse, "The Relationship of Love to Faith in St. John," *Theological Studies* 18 (1957):543-47.

14. Cf. Schnackenburg, *John*, pp. 396-97.

15. R. Bultmann, *The Gospel of John, a Commentary* (Philadelphia, 1971), p. 1 53.

16. Cf. Pss 23:1, 80:2; Is 40:11; Jer 31:9; Zech 11:4-13; and Ez 34, where a messianic motif is introduced, with the addition of the imagery of a Davidic shepherd to that of the divine shepherd.

17. For a good treatment of the significance of the Caiaphas episode, cf. C. H. Dodd, "The Prophecy of Caiaphas (Jn 11:47-53)," *Neotestamentica et Patristica* (Supplements to Novum Testamentum, VI) (Leiden), pp. 134-43.

18. Cf. Brown, *John, XIII-XXI*, pp. 766-67.

19. Dodd, *Interpretation*, p. 262.

20. Cf. Barrett, *John*, pp. 80-82.

21. Necessarily, this theme is treated very briefly here. For a fuller discussion, ef., besides the standard commentaries, F. M. Braun, *Mother of God's People* (New York, 1968), pp. 74-124; A. Feuillet, "L'heure de la femme (Jn 16:21) et l'heure de la Mère de Jésus (Jn 19:25-27)," *Biblica* 47 (1966):169-84, 361-80, 557-73; M. Zerwick, "The Hour of the Mother—John 19:25-27." *Bible Today* (1965), pp. 1187-94.

The Contemporaneity
of Christ's Passion in the
Epistles of Saint Paul

Barnabas Mary Ahern C.P.
Monastery of Saints John and Paul
Rome, Italy

Every character profile of St. Paul of the Cross emphasizes his constant, grateful remembrance of the passion of Christ. Devotion to the mystery of the cross gave direction to his life and prompted all his fundamental options. Obviously such devotedness meant something more than frequent mental recall of the events of the first Good Friday. It also involved full awareness that the passion of Christ is a perduring reality, ever present to men not only in the sufferings of his mystical body but also in its permanence and efficacy. All through the many years of his life, Paul found inspiration and strength in the principle *Crux stat dum orbs volvitur:* while the world spins or falters along its course, the crucified Christ is always present as the saving wisdom and power of God. Borrowing the phrase of Soren Kierkegaard, we may say that, for Paul, Christ on the cross was an "eternal contemporary."

Awareness of the passion as an ever-present mystery was not uniquely personal to the spirituality of this saint of the Crucified. Both before and after the time of Paul of the Cross, consciousness of this saving truth has been deeply rooted in authentic Christianity as the special legacy of Paul the Apostle. The conviction that the passion of Christ perdures forever is to the fore in his "great epistles" (1-2 Corinthians, Galatians, Romans) and in the "letters of the captivity" (Colossians, Ephesians). Study of these inspired apostolic writ-

ings is bound to give a deepened understanding of the
lifeline desire of Paul of the Cross: "May the passion
of Christ be always in our hearts."

The Ingrafting of Christ's Death into Pauline Faith

A significant difference separated the Apostle of the
Gentiles from the core group of Jesus' disciples who
shepherded the primitive community in Jerusalem. In
passing from the religion of Judaism to life in Christ,
the twelve had the benefit of several years' apprenticeship. Though they could hardly qualify as totally re-
ceptive novices, they rejoiced to see their master manifest God's goodness and listened appreciatively to his
self-revealing words; they marveled at the works of
God he performed and were so impressed by these
wonders that, at length, they formed and articulated
the conviction "Thou art the Christ" (Mk 8:29). The
road they traveled was often dark, but, with Jesus the
wayfarer as guide, they had enough light to look forward expectantly to the journey's end. In a sure but
clouded way, they were prepared for the moment of
arrival heralded on Easter Sunday and consummately
attained at Pentecost.

Paul had no share in this apprenticeship. If he heard
reports of the words and deeds of Jesus, he regarded
them as pretentious claims of an imposter. In his judgment the crucifixion was a penalty which Jesus justly
deserved for his blasphemous pose as Messiah. He
therefore found it abhorrent that some of his fellow
Jews should keep alive Jesus' pretentions by professing
faith in his resurrection. But at the very moment when
he strove to stamp out this infamy, Saul himself came
face to face with the Christ of glory. The encounter

blinded him with the brilliance of God's consummate self-revelation in the radiant person of Jesus, his Son and his Christ.

Unlike the twelve, Saul, the ardent Jew, was plummeted, without preparation, from the narrow world of the Old Covenant into the vast "new creation" which God brought to life in and through the resurrection of his crucified Son. At the gates of Damascus, he, whose life as a Jew was totally dedicated to the glory of Yahweh, was dumbfounded by the vision of this glory shining on the face of Jesus (cf. 2 Cor 4:6).

This experience gave such clarity and momentum to Paul's thoughts that it would seem his life and apostleship ever after should have centered on only one theme, "the Good News of glory of Christ who is the image of God" (2 Cor 4:4). The surprising fact that his letters give equal prominence to the death of Jesus suggests that at some time in his ministry, Paul's Damascus faith in the risen Christ was enriched with awareness of the meaning and efficacy of the passion.

When this development took place, and what divine lights and human reflection prompted it, cannot be known with certainty. It is always risky to trace Paul's spiritual aeneid along the guidelines of a seeming thought development in his correspondence. The fact that he lived seventeen years as an apostle before he wrote his first letter indicates that he had ample time to ponder and to grow. The additional fact that all his letters were occasional, -directed to the special needs and concerns of local churches, recommends caution in affirming that statements and silences in a given letter reveal the full mind of Paul at the moment of composition.

The resultant need to be wary in assigning definite

stages to his interior growth should not, however, cripple the study of doctrinal development in his literary corpus. Yet, even in this area, a student who looks for unilinear progress will be baffled by surprise when an unsuspected facet of glowing thought flashes forth from an unpromising text. This occurs especially in a study of his doctrine on the death of Christ.

The sermons of the Apostle recorded in St. Luke's recountal of the first and second missionary journeys (Acts 13:4 to 18:21) do not manifest any particular interest in the role of Christ's passion. The same must be said of Paul's first two letters, written to the Thessalonians during his second journey. Though he speaks of the death of Jesus in 1 Thess 2:15, his words are disappointing since he merely cites the example of Jesus (together with "the prophets" and "the churches of Judea") to show that every Christian must suffer.

With this scanty preparation, one is hardly ready for the surprise one finds in the first two chapters of 1 Corinthians. Here Paul forcefully reminds his converts that, in his apostolate among them, he is intent on "preaching the word of the cross"—and this at the very time when he was writing to the Thessalonians his noncommittal mention of Jesus' death. At Corinth, he was so aware that Christ crucified is "the power and wisdom of God" (1 Cor 1:24) that he boasts, in 1 Cor 2:2, "I decided to know nothing among you except Jesus Christ and him crucified." This manifesto bears remarkable similarity to his later insistence in his preaching on the prominence of Christ's resurrection: "What we preach is not ourselves, but Jesus Christ as Lord" (2 Cor 4:5). The impressive parallelism of these two statements, especially when read in context, shows that—for Paul at Corinth—the death of Jesus was comparable in importance to his resurrection.

The surprise occasioned by this sharp contrast between Paul's earlier silence and the forthright affirmations of 1 Cor 1-2 is accentuated by several passages in the letter to the Philippians, which, like 1 Corinthians, was probably written during the third missionary journey. A phrase in Phil 3:10 casually introduces, without explanation, the correlatives which lie at heart of Pauline soteriology: "the power of his resurrection and the fellowship of his sufferings."

More remarkable still is the liturgical hymn which Paul quotes in Phil 2:6-11. Mention of the servant theme in vv. 7-8 evokes the early preaching apostolate of the twelve and their disciples (Acts 3:13, 26; 7:52; 8:30-35; cf. Is 53:11-12). It also echoes the preoccupation of the Jerusalem church with the humiliating death of Jesus as the chief obstacle to Jewish belief in his resurrection. When and by whom this hymn was composed are impossible to ascertain. What is of paramount importance is Paul's implicit approval of its contents in using it to express his own thoughts. By introducing this hymn, he affirms his conviction that God's saving work includes both Jesus' death and resurrection as constitutive elements of one and the same redemptive mystery.

These words about the death of Christ in Paul's early correspondence are unfolded in his later writings. These epistles make clear that his attention is always fixed on the risen Christ; at the same time, however, they show equal awareness that the Lord of glory transforms the lives of men by the blood of his cross.

Paul's Perspective: Scriptural and Theological

The phrase "blood of his cross" might suggest that

the Apostle's letters provide material for a typical nineteenth-century manual of devotion to the passion of Christ. To study the Pauline epistles with this expectancy is to be disappointed, but this does not mean that manuals of piety are without value. In recalling and honoring the historical sufferings of Jesus, Christian saints and writers of many centuries have effectively cultivated an apt means for strengthening the response of human hearts to the redemptive sufferings which Paul himself has called the eminent manifestation of God's love (cf. Rom 5:8).

If in his writings Paul has consistently avoided such realistic recall of the passion of Christ, a plausible reason may explain this silence. His ever vivid memory of the Damascus vision of Jesus as the glorious Messiah could have made it painful for him to recreate the passion mentally, with its revolting scenes of cruelty and anguish. As a contemporary of the first Good Friday, Paul was familiar with the physical and psychical agonies of Roman crucifixion, and, more poignant still, he could not forget his own complacent approval of the agony of Jesus. But, independent of explanatory reasons, the fact is that Paul confined his attention to the salvific realities of the cross, that is, the divine elements which give the death of Jesus its perennial meaning and efficacy in God's work of saving the world. Only this kind of faith-insight can provide the true perspective for every kind of prayerful pondering of the historical passion. Only by sharing Paul's vision does one come to see how this event of the past still lives in the present.

In his reflections on the divine realities of the passion, Paul leaned heavily on the typologies of the Old

Testament. The salvation history of Israel provided him with analogies and a medium of language for understanding and explaining God's eminent saving work in and through Jesus. The Old Testament emphases on redemption, the reconciling power of blood, the justice of God—these are the typologies which Paul used most often in probing the meaning of Jesus' death. For some uncertain reason, he made little use of the Isaian typology of the "Servant of Yahweh," even though this theme was to the fore in the kerygma and catechesis of the Jerusalem community. It is also significant that Paul does not unfold in detail the full potentialities of his preferred Old Testament analogies. Thus almost too swiftly, in two brief verses (Rom 3:24-25), he likens God's justifying action in Christ both to the "redemption" and to the "expiatory rite" of Israel, without any explanation of the riches these two comparisons contain. Of special surprise is the fact that his use of the Passover analyogy is confined to a bare allusion (cf. 1 Cor 5:7).

Perhaps this reserve is due to Paul's confidence that previous oral teaching rendered explanation unnecessary. He was writing for a well-instructed audience, long familiar with the Old Testament language and thought patterns which were being used in the New Testament catechesis. But it is also possible that, in speaking of the eminent saving work of God, Paul was unwilling to confine his teaching to the procrustean bed of an Old Covenant, which was only a "shadow of things to come" (Col 2:17). In actual fact, some of Paul's major insights were stated by him, and can be understood by us, without any need for referral to the Old Testament. As he sets forth these insights, the

Apostle writes as one whose gaze is fixed solely on the redemptive mystery itself.

Chief Elements in Paul's Doctrine of the Cross

Schooled in the theocentric faith of Israel, Paul could not think of the redemptive mystery except in the light of what he considered a first truth: God himself was the chief actor both on Good Friday and Easter Sunday. To stress that God alone was author of Jesus' resurrection, he always writes either "God raised Jesus" or "Jesus was raised [by God]"; only on one occasion (in 1 Thess 4:14) does he depart from this usage. Naturally, therefore, when Paul speaks of Jesus' passion and death, he emphasizes this same divine causality. Far from being a fortuitous prelude to messianic glorification, the death of Jesus is presented by Paul as involving the wise plan and saving power of the Father (cf. 1 Cor 1:17-25, 2:7-9; Rom 5:6-8, 8:3, 32). The Apostle, therefore, is totally in character when, writing of the whole ensemble of Jesus' redemptive death and resurrection, he utters the firm conviction that "it is all God's work. It was God who reconciled us to himself through Christ" (2 Cor 5:17-18).

This factor of divine causality is of special significance if we are to understand the contemporaneity of Christ's passion. Because Jesus' death occurred at a given moment in time, the suggestion of its perduring efficacy would be incomprehensible to the man who overlooks Paul's emphasis on God at work with the fullness of his divine power. Not so St. Thomas Aquinas; he was one who grasped Paul's thought perfectly. In discussing the efficiency of Christ's passion in every age of time, he explains the humanly unexplainable with words that faithfully crystallize St. Paul's conviction:

> Christ's Passion in relation to his flesh is consistent with the infirmity which he took upon himself, but in relation to the Godhead it draws infinite might from it . . . Therefore all Christ's actions and sufferings operate instrumentally in virtue of his Godhead for the salvation of men [*S. Theol.* III, Q 49 *ad finem* and ad 1].

This recognition of God's power at work in the passion is intimately connected with a second factor in Paul's thought. The Apostle affirms that the death of Jesus was totally inspired by the *agape* of Father and Son, that is, by their strong, tender, and saving love. The generosity of the Father in delivering his Son to the cross and the devoted obedience of Jesus to his Father's saving will were equally prompted by their mutual loving concern for man's redemption (Rom 5:5-11, 8:31-39; Gal 2:20). This mercy, which "surpasses all knowledge" (Eph 3:19), acted as the sole directive of the divine power at work in Jesus' death, thereby making his cross the efficacious source of limitless blessings for all men of all ages. Only the Spirit of God knows and can make known the profound depths and vast reaches of this efficacy (1 Cor 2:7-16). Face to face with so eminent a mystery of divine love, Paul speaks of it as "the ineffable *charis*" —the gift of God that beggars all description (2 Cor 8:9, 9:15). The Apostle's characteristic response to this divine largesse is not the probing of analytic theology but a heartful paean of exultant "boasting" and thankfulness (cf. Rom 5:1-11, 8:31-39, 11:33-36, Eph 1:3-10).

Such worshipful awe before the mystery of God's power serving his boundless love accounts for a third factor in Paul's theology of the passion. Instead of trying to dissect all that is contained in the mind-baffling mercy of God and his Christ, Paul is content simply to proclaim its certain reality. This fact explains the disappointing silences of 1 Cor 1-4. Though these chapters suggest much, with their boastful affirmations of the "power and wisdom" of Jesus crucified, they present no clarifying explanation. Even when Paul tries to unfold the mystery of redemption in Rom 1-8, he is forced to speak with the inadequate language of Old Testament typologies and earthy analogies. Conscious of the innate poverty of his words, he confesses frankly to the Romans: "I am speaking in human terms because of your natural limitations" (Rom 6:19). Throughout this treatment of how God makes man righteous through the death and resurrection of Jesus (Rom 1-8), the Apostle is far more intent on stressing the need for man's response than on preparing an exhaustive analysis of the mystery which surpasses human comprehension.

This emphasis on human response is so characteristic of Paul's treatment of redemption that Rudolf Bultmann describes his writings as a study of Christian anthropology. In a certain sense this statement is warranted: the Apostle shows a predominant concern with the effects of Jesus' death and resurrection in the lives of those who respond with faith. But this very anthropology provides a revelatory glimpse of the extent and riches of the powerful saving love with which God works in and through the death-resurrection of his Son. Therefore it is chiefly by pondering what Paul says about the effects of the passion in man that one comes to see dimly, as in a dull mirror, the ineffable efficacy of the passion itself.

The Passion of Jesus as the Death of a Corporate Person

For Paul, these three elements of divine causality, saving love, and spiritual efficacy are the operative constitutives of the messiahship of Jesus, whom God raised from the dead. Far from being a mere resuscitation to earthly life, as in the experience of Lazarus and the daughter of Jairus, the resurrection of God's Son was a total transformation of his human mode of existence. After the weakness of his incarnate life upon earth, he was enriched in every fiber of his humanness with the power of a glorious messianic enthronization. Speaking for the twelve, Peter proclaimed this fact on the day of Pentecost: "Let all the house of Israel know most certainly that God has made this Jesus whom you crucified both Lord and Christ" (Acts 2:36). From the moment of his Damascus vision, Paul accepted this same truth with all his heart and proclaimed it ceaselessly (Acts 13:32-33, 17:31; 1 Thes 1:9-10; Rom 1:3-4; etc.). For him, the very Jesus who died lives now and always with the Father as his messianic Son, through whom alone men gain salvation.

This faith of Paul is luminous with his own distinctive insight. Contrary to Jewish expectancy of a preternatural messianic intervention of God, Paul conjured with the stark fact of history that God accomplished the salvation of the world in and through one who, like other men, was "born of a woman, born under the Law" (Gal 4:4). Though this salvation must be attributed to God as its author, his wise plan had ordained that he would "reconcile us to himself through Christ" (2 Cor 5:18), a man integrally human, who suffered, died, and rose from the tomb.

This death and resurrection, though totally personal to Jesus, were at the same time God's chosen way of fulfilling his pledge of salvation. Through the human history of his Messiah, God reconciled the world to himself, made it a "new creation," and changed lead-footed time into a constant "now," alive with the *"kairos*-time" of full messianic opportunity (2 Cor 5:14-6:2). Using the thought patterns of the Old Testament, Paul saw that Jesus, as the promised Messiah, was not only a man like all others, possessing his own individuality, but also a "corporate person." This means, in the language of today, that the human history of Jesus has power to become the history of every man. To state this in another way: The messianic salvation which came to the world through Jesus has its total source and operative form in the experiences of his death and resurrection.

Unique Efficacy of the Passion

The fact that Paul sees Jesus as a divnely empowered corporate person provides the basic reason for his affirmations about the distinctive efficacy of the passion. Without doubt, the Apostle sees the death of Christ as always inseparably joined with the resurrection, both because Easter Sunday crowns the total finality of Good Friday and because the person and love of the crucified Jesus are identical with the person and love of the risen Lord of glory. At the same time, however, Paul knows that death and resurrection were for Jesus two entirely different human experiences, each with its own distinctive contribution to the messianic work of liberation and union.

This does not mean that Paul always clearly demarcates this distinctiveness. Time and again the compelling orientation of his thoughts to the living Christ of glory will blur the precise efficacy of the two aspects of the redemptive mystery. Analysis and distinction are not characteristic of full-hearted love; and Paul was a lover. At the same time he was an apostle who found it needful to spell out for his frail Christians the specific exigencies of the death and resurrection they were called to share. We are indebted, therefore, to Paul's backsliding converts for those luminous portions of his letters where he sets out in detail the precise meaning and efficacy of Jesus' death.

For Paul this death was, above all else, God's work of liberation—for Jesus himself and, through him, for all men. In the language of the Apostle, the bondage from which Jesus was freed was the human mode of experience in *sarx* (i.e., mortal humanness), in a world of sin, and in subservience to the law. In a sense, all men who die cease living the earth-bound modes which trammel life with weakness, defect, and the resultant inability to fulfill even beneficent laws. But Jesus' death was something different from the universal death experience of ceasing to live as a man of this world.

Paul does not give a lengthy explanation of all that made the death of Jesus a unique human experience; but when he writes of this, his words are finely honed. He speaks of the passion as Jesus' act of total devoted obedience to the saving will of the Father (Phil 2:7-8; 2 Cor 1:19-20; Rom 5:19). By this he means that Jesus accepted the nadir of the death experience with a heart that beat in total human harmony with the Father's love for men (cf. Rom 8:32-34, 5:6-9). A death like this, prompted by total surrender to the Father's will and instinct with the power of God's own love, broke all the bonds which had previously held Christ fast in the weakness of human life upon earth, thus liberating him for the heavenly life of untrammeled union with the Father. Such a death as this had to be followed by resurrection, the welcoming embrace with which the Father received his Son and endowed his humanness with the full saving power of messiahship.

For Paul, therefore, the death of Jesus was not merely the cessation of life upon earth. It was the breaking of this world's bonds under the impact of love—a severance that freed his human life for perfect transformation and for perfect union with his Father in bestowing upon men the messianic gift of the Spirit. Paul's best word to express the wonder of this mystery is his recurring phrase "the blood of Christ."

In Hebrew sacrifice, the blood which contained the life of the beast-victim and symbolized the life of God's people was poured on the altar or on the "mercy seat" (*kapporeth*) of the Ark to signify both Israel's purification and its renewed union with Yahweh, who was believed to be present with his holy and saving mercy. But the sacrifice of beasts was at best an encouraging symbol, urging the people to offer Yahweh the true penitence of their hearts. Only Jesus could perfectly accomplish what these blood sacrifices weakly prefigured. The life that was in his blood was the life of God's own Son, offered on the cross with the devotedness of a human heart which responded with unique fidelity to the loving will of the Father.

Such a death meant total liberation for Jesus from the pull of earthiness, that he might live totally with the freedom of the Spirit. At the same time, the theandric and vicarious character of his death experience made this exodus an event with divine power to become the actual experience of every man. The cross and the blood are forever; whoever believes in Jesus and the ever-present power of his death is able to make his own the words of St. Paul, "With Christ I am nailed to the cross; and I live, now not I, but Christ lives in me" (Gal 2:20). If today liberty and liberation have become the passionate ideal of many, let those who use these words understand clearly that there is only one authentic kind of emancipation: it is the "freedom for which Christ has set us free' (Gal 5:1)—under condition of our readiness to share the liberating experience of his death on the cross.

Liberation through the Spirit

To some, the phrase "sharing Christ's death" may suggest the Christian's need to imitate the virtues with which he died. Undoubtedly this is an essential part of man's liberation. But, curiously enough, St. Paul himself hardly adverts to the exemplary character of Christ's conduct. He is far more concerned with the effective way in which Christ's death touches the history of every man at the deepest core of his personality. Were Paul to have dealt with the passion as imitable, his concern would have centered on the sufferings of Christ as a historical event of the past. Instead, he centers attention on the way in which the passion, as a perennial reality, enters into and transforms the lives of men in the present.

He describes this in language which is realistic and picturesque. In his teaching, the man who becomes a Christian breaks the earthly bonds which hold him back from God, but only by being "baptized into the death of Christ" (Rom 6:3-4) and by being "buried into his death" (Col 2:12). More than this, and using an "I" that speaks for every Christian, Paul affirms that he himself has been "nailed to the cross with Christ" (Gal 2:20), not only at baptism, but also through the whole of life. He says, too, that "those who belong to Christ Jesus have crucified their flesh with its propensities and cravings" (Gal 5:24). Just as the cross freed Jesus from earth's bondage to weakness and liberated him from the world's atmosphere of sin, so too, by sharing the experience of Christ's death, the Christian is set free from all earthly blight to enjoy the liberty and holiness of intimate union with God. Dying each day with Christ, he anticipates, upon earth, that joy and peace which will be his when physical death brings its ultimate share in the dying of Jesus. It is this prospect of total liberation which Paul alludes to on the only two occasions when he speaks of his own death (Phil 1:21-23; 2 Cor 5:1-10).

These affirmations of the Apostle might be interpreted as merely figurative expressions of the conformity to Christ which the Christian must accomplish by his own efforts. Interpreted in this way, Paul's doctrine would be disappointing, since it would reduce the efficacy of Christ's passion to mere exemplarity. His teachig would even be discouraging, since it would demand of the Christian strenuous Pelagian efforts, which, due to innate human weakness, are always bound to fail.

In actual fact, peering into the very depths of God's saving work, Paul has discovered the consummate mystery of the present efficacy of the passion of Christ. He sees how the boundless love of the Father and his Son have found a way to make Jesus' experience on the cross an ever-present reality in the lives of Christians who are members of his body. This work of infinite power and love is accomplished through the Holy Spirit. Given to each Christian in baptism, the Spirit not only unites him to the person of Jesus but enables him to experience "the power of Christ's resurrection and the fellowship of his sufferings" (Phil 3:10). This does not mean that the Spirit renews, in a superficial material way, the fleshly crucifixion of Jesus or his blood-shedding on the cross. Instead, he forges a bond between the Crucified and the Christian in a much deeper and more intimate way. By transforming the human heart with Christ's obedience and love, he makes the Christian Christ's "other self" and renews in him the liberation of Jesus' own death on the cross.

This is what Paul means when he speaks of the Christian's bearing "the sufferings of Christ" (2 Cor 1:5; Col 1:24) and of himself marked with the wounds of Christ (Gal 6:17). Made a member of the body-self of Christ and filled with his love by the action of the indwelling Holy Spirit, the follower of Jesus shares so fully in the redemptive mystery of the cross that he lives no longer of his own resources but only under the impulse of the Spirit of Jesus—the Jesus who relives his passion in him. Christ's love, given by the Spirit to the members of his body, renews in them the liberation achieved by his death; it frees from all sin, dissolves weakness into virtue, and substitutes for the external yoke of law the impelling desire to do always the things which please the Father.

All this is the work of the Spirit, who is himself the very power and love of God. It is significant, therefore, that St. Paul concludes his long discussion of the redemptive work of Christ (in Rom 1–7) with

the climactic eighth chapter, in which he unfolds the
role of the Spirit in the life of the Christian. Without
this chapter, all that he has written about "dying
with Christ," all that he has taught about the power
of Christ's blood to cleanse and liberate, all his apt
use of his characteristic *syn*-compounds ("with-dying
with Christ," "with-being crucified," "with-being buried")—all this would be, at best, a beautiful figurative expression of what Christian life could be through
man's effort to imitate the crucified Jesus. But with
this chapter and its wondrous description of the work
of the Spirit, Paul lays bare the deep foundation of
a faith-insight far more precious. In Romans 8 he
makes clear that the boundless power and love of God
have made it possible, through the Holy Spirit, that
the passion of Christ should be not only the exemplary
cause of man's liberation but also its present, perennial,
and everoperative efficient cause.

L'Envoi

This faith-insight of Paul the Apostle illumines and
gives substance to the spirituality of St. Paul of the
Cross. In his letters to those who sought spiritual
counsel, he constantly urged frequent thought and
grateful remembrance of the sufferings of Christ. But
he always saw this devotedness as the way to grow in
awareness of a deeper truth. Memory of the sacred
passion makes one realize that the love and power of
God, like a vast ocean, endure forever. Immersed in
this sea, the Christian relives the experience of Christ's
death. He is freed from the bonds of earth, purified
of sin, and united to the will of God in perfect fidelity. And with this daily dying, he lives more and

more the life of Christ's resurrection. For Paul of the Cross, as for Paul the Apostle, Christ's love, given to us by the Spirit, is the meaning of it all.